Growing Up on a One Mule Farm

William (Bill) Jefferson Taylor
Author-Pastor-Evangelist
Wingate NC

Foreword by
Rev. David Gales- Pastor Emeritus
Plaza Baptist Church, Charlotte, NC

authorHOUSE®

AuthorHouse™
1663 Liberty Drive
Bloomington, IN 47403
www.authorhouse.com
Phone: 1-800-839-8640

© *2009 William (Bill) Jefferson Taylor. All rights reserved.*

No part of this book may be reproduced, stored in a retrieval system, or transmitted by any means without the written permission of the author.

First published by AuthorHouse 11/19/2009

ISBN: 978-1-4490-5338-3 (e)
ISBN: 978-1-4490-5337-6 (sc)

Library of Congress Control Number: 2009912599

Printed in the United States of America
Bloomington, Indiana

This book is printed on acid-free paper.

Foreword

I have known Brother Bill Taylor for over 40 years as a fellow pastor and close friend. Bill's preaching has been greatly used by God in seeing many souls come into the kingdom of God. Wherever he has gone as pastor or an evangelist, souls have been won to Christ. Robin, his and Eva's daughter, was my organist at Plaza Baptist in Charlotte for many years, until the Lord called Rick and Robin to the mission field with Overseas Missionary Fellowship.

Bill has been a golfing buddy through the years. I have cherished the time we have spent together. One of my highlights in golf was being in the foursome with him when he had a hole –in-one. He is a dear friend that means so much to me.

Rev. David Gales- Pastor Emeritus
Plaza Baptist Church ,Charlotte, NC
32 years as pastor before retirement

Contents

Dedication	xi
Preface	xiii
Introduction	xv
Old Tob	1
The One Mule Farm	2
Procters Bend	4
School Days	7
Back To The Bend	8
Whisky Still	11
River Fishing	12
The Scare Of My Life	14
Syrup Mill	15
Leaving The Bend Behind	16
Back To The One Mule Farm	17
Liberty School	18
The Toy Train	19
Possum Hunting	20
Squrell And Rabbit Hunting	21
More Liberty School	23
Tornado Hits Gainesville	24
Liberty Baptist Church	25
Singing School	28
Lightening Strikes	28
Truck Wagons	30
Summer Time	31

Our Two Dogs	32
Catching Wild Hogs	34
Fred's Bull, And Calves	34
Comic Books	35
A Barb Wire Fence	37
Lovingood Bridge	38
Cotton To Chickens	40
Baseball	43
Pearl Harbor	45
On The Way Home From Church	47
Uncle Bill Jenkins	49
Christmas Fun	50
Mr. Lawernce Towsend's Store	51
Sanky Hughes Store And Mill	53
Lumping School	53
Dawsonville High School	55
Uncles	56
Uncles That Married Grandma And Grandpa's Daughters	57
My Grand Parents On My Mothers'side Of The Family	59
Sad Times	61
Acworth High School	62
Basketball	63
Bell Aircraft Basketall	65
The Black Cat's Kitten	66
Honey Bees	67
Riding To Town In The Wagon	68
Uncle Bill Cantrell	69

Canton Georgia	71
Hawks Can't Count	72
Santa Clause	73
Stealing Watermellons	74
Black Berry Time	76
Picking Cotton	78
Grandpa Taylor	79
Grandma Taylor	81
A Soul Winner	82
A Personal Word From The Author	84
A Sad Time In My Life	85
What Others Have Written About Eva	87
Meet The Author	91
Church Web Sites	95
Recommending	97

Dedication

I would like to dedicate these writing in memory of my older brother, James. Who left his bride to take his place with many who did the same. To defeat the Germans and bring about peace in Europe. Many paid the supreme price along with him, with their deaths, that we might enjoy the freedom we have today.

Also in memory of my loving and beautiful wife, Eva, of over sixty years, before the Lord called her home. We had such a wonderful life together. Words can not describe how much I miss her, but one day I will see her again.

PREFACE

I came to realize that the day would come when my children, grand children, and great grand children would know very little about my early childhood and teen age years. At the urging of my daughters, Diane and Robin, I made the decision to put some words in print. In so doing I am able to reveal something about myself, and some things of my kindred on Dad's side of my family, and on Mom's side. Some that have no relation as kindred, just friends.

Then there are true stories that you will enjoy. I believe they are informative and some will cause the reader to laugh.

Bill's Mother

INTRODUCTION

When you have lived more than eighty years, there are many things that this generation knows nothing about. But there are some things that we appreciated, and some that we have experienced that makes us more thankful . I wonder if those "good old days" were not so bad. Life was hard, but the simplicity of it causes us to look back. Then wonder how the youth of this day would respond if the clock was reversed.

I know it was bound to have been hard on my parents. There were four children, and Mom and Dad to feed and clothe . I think they did a great job at it. I will have to say a word of praise for old "Tob" our one mule on the one mule farm.

I think you will enjoy reading what I will share with you who have never known what it was like in those days. No one was talking in our home about the "great depression" although we were living in it. We were thankful that we had a mule and a small farm , and never went hungry and without clothing.

Bill's Father

Old Tob

    I guess I should introduce you to OLD TOB. Since he was the one mule on the ONE MULE FARM . Finally he got some help when we were able to buy Mandy after several years . But most of all those years, OLD TOB carried the load.

    He was an educated mule. I started following him when I was I guess about eight. Once you established where you wanted him to walk. He would walk there. You were not having to gee or haw. Mule language, that he understood, also get up and whoa, and come around. He also could keep time. When Mom would ring the dinner bell. You city slickers call it lunch. It was dinner and then supper. But OLD TOB, knew it was time to eat. And he was not going to plow another row when he got back to the end of the row toward the house. He was going to go get something to eat and drink.

    Old Tob was over twenty years and still spry. A truck came by on the gravel highway with a tarp flapping on it and he was frighten and ran away dragging the sled he was pulling for Dad to the field. He stopped maybe a hundred yards later and waited on Dad to catch up. I don't think he liked kids. I had hold of his front trying to get him to raise his front foot. He reached down and bit me on my leg, breaking the skin. I had seen Dad get him to do that when he was checking his shoes.

    It was a sad day when we sold OLD TOB. We were moving from Dawson County Georgia, to Cherokee County. And he wasn't going with us.

The One Mule Farm

The farm was in two sections, divided by the gravel highway and woods that were owned by neighbors. One section where we lived was used for a small orchard , a garden , watermelon and cantaloupe patches, and corn. The rest was pasture. We did not have a stream on either section. So water for the animals , and yard chickens had to be drawn by rope and bucket from the well, which was a deep one.

Dad had purchased the farm from Tony Hughes, a neighbor. He had saved to pay for the farm and when he went to the bank to get the money to pay for it. The bank was closed and he lost everything he had in the bank. Dillard Elliott, loaned him the money to pay for the farm. Dad was able to receive a loan from the Federal Land Bank to pay Dillard. During those days it was a struggle just to pay the interest on the loan when it came due each year. Mom and Dad made the decision to sell the farm to his youngest brother, Henry, and we moved to Cherokee county to farm with Mom's nephew, Fred Willbanks.

We first moved to a farm house between Ballground and Canton a few hundreds yards from the home in which I was born. I will never forget my first day at school at Ballground. What ever the Cherokee Indians called it, meant Ballground. What kind of ball they played there I have no idea.

There was this bully on my first day at school who challenged me for a fight at recess. I wanted to take him on. But my Mother had already a few years before giving me a trashing for fighting. When we lived across the gravel highway from the two room school. A boy cursed me as we came across the highway from school. I put my books in our mail box and chased him down and threw him in a ditch. I landed on top of him and was working him over when someone grabbed my collar and pulled me off of him. To my surprise it was Mom and she had a switch in her hand and switched by legs all the way to the house. She told me if I got into another fight she would whip me again. So I did not fight the bully. When I got home from school I told Dad what happen. He asked me if I could whip this bully. I told him I would have no trouble whipping him. He said whip him and I will see that your Mom doesn't whip you. I could not wait till the next day for recess. I can see it now as we came out of the class rooms on to the yard. There he was calling me a coward. He had a bunch of students behind him wanting to see a fight. I walked to pass him as if I was ignoring him. Then I gave him a sucker punch in his belly and he went down. My cousin Tilman was in the group, he was encouraging the fight. I reached for him and he ran .The teacher came out and made us come in and she paddled us in our hands with a ruler. I had tough hands as a farm boy, did not phase me. I had no more problems with him or any of the others.

Fred Willbanks

I was glad when we moved from Ballground. While we were there we worked at a dairy for Fred Willbanks, Mom's nephew. I had to get up at dawn and milk . I think it was seven cows. They were call strippers. We did not save the milk to drink, the cows were soon to give birth to calves. We always had a bunch of new born calves, more than we had strippers. We would put their heads down in the milk bucket and put our fingers in their mouths and they would suck on our fingers and in so doing suck up milk. We would also let them nurse the cows of what was left. two per cow. Then that all had to be done again before dark.

Procters Bend

Our next stop was in Procters Bend, located below Canton Georgia. It was named that because the river made a tremendous bend almost a half circle . Some of the riches land you could desire that did not get flooded when the river was out of its banks. Fred Willbanks , Mom's (half) nephew, son of her half sister, had a deal with the Georgia Power Company to be the care taker of this land and other land. They had purchased the land from owners for the purpose of building the Altoona Dam near Cartersville and most of this land would be under water when it was finished, what a shame, but I guess they needed the electricity that it produces. I think they paid him a dollar per acre. He could farm the land. So we moved into a fabulous , and beautiful old plantation home in the middle of the bend , up on the hill. With the farm land around us. We did have some neighbors that lived in what were share cropper homes, the Mundays and the Cowans. Uncle Ed , Dad's brother, also moved to one of the homes. I don't remember how long he lived there, or when he moved there.

Our deal with Fred, was he would plow the fields with his tractors, plant them, furnished everything. Then we were to cultivate the crops ,harvest the crops, and we would get one third of the yield. The big level field was planted in Cotton, about 50 to 75 acres. Which no doubt would have produced at least more than one half a bale per acre. But the weather did not do us a favor. It rained so much and the crab grass took over the cotton field . We had to just abandon much of the field. Had to go in with hoes and dig out the grass. We hired hoe hands to hoe the cotton and to help pick it. James my older brother and I did the plowing with a mule and a horse. We had other fields of corn separate from the large track. We had a large garden spot behind the house. I remember the big collard path. I guess I remember it since I hated collards, but Mom cooked them and we ate them.

We also broke some horses for Fred that he had bought that had never been hitched or ridden. And some of them had never been shod. To shoe them they had to be strapped where they could not kick the blacksmith. I remember one particular one that wasn't wild, I got on it bare back and he started out across the field with me on his back. I wanted him to stop and I started pulling on the reigns. He just got faster and when he slowed down to jump a terrace, I jumped off of him. He went a few feet and stopped and turned around facing me. So happened that he had been trained as a roping horse in a rodeo. He was waiting for me to tie the calf legs together, but there was no calf, but a lot of laughs from several of those who were watching.

Talk about riding, it was coming up a thunder cloud and James and I headed for the barn, left our gears in the field and took off to the barn. I was on a mule he was on a horse. I was ahead of him and he passed me just before we arrived at the barn he hit the mule on its behind with his bridle strap and she started running and fell down and I went out over her head , head first. James was laughing so hard he fell off of the horse. James would take one of the horses that had never been broken to be rode into to a new plowed field, get on it and whip it with his straw hat until it would stop running. He had to get it where it would not buck. We had this city drug store cowboy that came to help us hoe. He wanted to ride one of these horses that was about half broke. He was warned not to get on it. But he insisted, bare back, we never owned a saddle. Don't ever try to ride a horse with a saddle until it is completely trained to accept a rider. So this fellow jumps on this horse in a hard field road. And when he did . it raised up on its hind legs, then on its front legs and jumped side ways and he made a three point landing on his behind in the middle of the road, with a bruised butt and a lot of folks laughing at him. I don't remember how many of those horses we broke. Come to think about it, Fred never paid us for breaking them. As soon as we got one broke he would take it to a sale and sell it. But breaking them was fun. We always kept one great big horse, Maud. She had been a logging horse. She walked so slow. We would hitch her with a wild one and the wild one would be jumping around getting its feet out of the traces , and after pulling all the load and old Maud, the wild one would settle down. This is how we broke them to plow as a team. Speaking of hoe help. we had this woman that came to help us hoe. I mentioned to Mom that she was a good hoer. Mom said don't use that word to describe her , say hoe hand. I did not know that I was describing the personal character of a woman. Well I guess I knew , but I did not realize how it sounded .

I remember that one night we were playing set back, a card game, the Mondays and the Taylors, when Dad said I bet there is a dozen possums in those persimmons trees a few yards from our house. So we got our flash lights and slipped down to the grove and then ran you could hear the possums that were on the ground running through the leaves and when we shinned the lights up in the trees there were 49 possums in those trees, I would say 50 but I would not tell a lie for one possum, ha-ha, think maybe four or five, we let them be, and returned to our card game. Don't remember the rules of the game, maybe someone does.

One thing I hated about the Bend was cutting corn stalks with a hoe and pilling them to burn to get the field ready to plant the next spring. What would happen was that the hoe did not cut the stalk clean and it pulled up the roots and you are trying to carry an arm full of stalks with the roots hanging on the end with mud.

The big house we lived in had so many rooms that we did not furnish some of them. We used some to store our cotton until we carried it to the gen. Cotton was brought from the field in large burlap sheets tied. When it was carried to a gen the sheets were empted in a closed truck bed and a big vacuum about a foot in diameter sucked up the cotton into the gen where the seeds were removed and then the cotton bailed in burlap with metal binders around it. Most bails would weight from 400 to 500 lbs. The seed was sold to make cotton seed meal for feed. Some seed were kept for planting. For some of you that don't know history, Eli Whitney invented the cotton gen.

We had to hire a lot of cotton pickers. I remember that Gale Hulsey a cousin, from Dawson County came and picked cotton. Maybe some more came. I remember her for two reasons. She and I went possum hunting with some friends one night, and she and I were picking cotton in the field . She wasn't doing so hot at it. I was putting cotton in her pick sack all along, and when we weight up for the day, she had picked more than I had. I got an earful from Dad. Gale was my third cousin , her mother Annie Hulsey was Dad's first cousin, daughter of Cunnie Patterson, Grandpa Jeff's sister.

School Days

The years we lived in the Bend, after we moved from Ballground. I am not sure, maybe three. Lot of things happened that I can't put a time table on . I know we moved to the Bend in the winter time and Betty and I walked three miles to Dry Branch School, a one room school. It was winter and cold at times. James our older brother had stayed in Dawson county until the school year was over. We had one teacher . The teacher had only one arm. He tried to whip Levi Long one day . Levi punched him in the chest, ran out the door and never went back. . Levi was a few years older than me. Betty , my sister, walked with me, she was in the third grade. I remember as we walked to school one morning of seeing where some dogs had been fighting all up and down the side of the road. I started looking at their tracks and found a dead bobcat that they had killed. I cut off two of its feet and mailed one to Tunney Gazaway my closest friend back in Dawson county. He wasn't at that time able to attend school. I think he had something like

Polio. Mr. Blankenship was the name of the teacher. He was the dumbest teacher I ever had. They closed the school at the close of the school year and we went then to New Bethel across the river about four miles from the bridge . We only had to walk about a mile to catch a bus ride to the school. It was in a pickup truck . The bed had a cover built over it with benches on each side . There was not very many of us that rode it . I remember a fight I had in the back of the bus. Of course it had a door at the back that was closed when we were moving and opened to let us out or in.

The Satterfields, not related to Eva, lived in the brick house that we moved into later, after they had moved. One of the Satterfield twins, they had two sets of twins, and more children. He acted like he was going to whisper something in my ear and when he got up close to my ear he spit in my ear. I grabbed him around the neck with my left arm and punched him in the face with my right fist . Well, he did not show up for school for a day or two. And when he did he looked like he had been worked over . I guess his twin sister, Thelma, told his parents what started the fight.

Back To The Bend

I enjoyed living in the Bend , even though we had no indoor plumbing or electricity. But there were some bad days. Dad got sick. His toe on his right foot turned black and begin to pain him awful. His trips to the doctor in Canton did not help, after spending 28 days total ,not in one trip, in the hospital they finally amputated his big toe and the ball of his foot. They figured out later that it was a bone chip that was pressing against a nerve and also cutting off blood flow to the toe.

They thought that it happened a long time before when a mule stepped on his foot. Here is a home remedy that Mom concocted up that help in the healing of the wound . She made a polis of persimmon bark and applied it to the wound. The bark was not the outside bark, but the thin moist bark inside the hard bark. It would draw out the pus and it soon healed. But Dad was never able to plow for a long time And limited on how much he could do for a while. But it was wonderful when he go rid of the pain.

    I have already mentioned the garden spot behind our house and the collards. Behind the garden was some real rich ground and we had planted cotton in it. I liked it because it had all kinds of small smooth marble size rocks in it that I could use in my sling shot, which we called a flip. I remember getting in an argument with by brother James, he picked up rock about the size of an egg and threw it at me and it hit me on the head. Didn't hurt much as it wasn't a direct hit. But I scared the daylights out of him . I fell down between the two cotton rows and stated kicking He grabbed me and started shaking me till I started laughing . In that same cotton patch I had hid between the rows and there was a chicken hawk circling overhead. I had dad's single shot shotgun and I was going to shoot it. Dad had bought that shot gun from a neighbor, George Scott, back in Dawson county . He gave him five dollars for it. Mr. Scott one day let a man borrow it to shoot some squirrels , but that wasn't what he wanted it for, he shot himself. Mr. Scott did not want to have it in his house. The hammer on the gun was so hard to cock that I would have to place the butt of the gun on the ground and use the heal of my hand to cock the hammer. That was what I was doing when my hand slipped off the hammer before I got it back enough to cock it and the gun went off. Now here is one for the believe it or not. When it fired it killed the hawk circling over head. Now see if you can top that. Here is another one. Before we left the one mule farm. The family and others were picking cotton in the field across the highway and the woods. We had a cotton storage building that we stored the cotton in until we had enough to take to the gen . My younger brother was an invalid for a few years before he was able to walk.

I was to watch after him. He would be in the cotton building on a quilt. I would just be fooling around outside. I heard our dog barking running a rabbit coming strait toward me. I just stood stiff as a board . My legs a few inches apart. When that rabbit came and ran between my legs and I caught it. I begin to holler , " I caught a rabbit" over and over. They did not believe me till I showed them the rabbit. Here is another rabbit story it happened in a cotton patch in the Bend. The dog was running a rabbit and it was coming strait toward me. I started looking for a rock for my flip. In this large field it did not have any rocks. I finally found one scaly rock, about the size and shape of a quarter. I stood real still with my flip cocked and when it got a few feet from me I let it go. It did go strait and hit the rabbit in the nose and it fell. I picked it up and whacked it on the back of its neck and took it and showed it to those who were in the field not far from me.

In the Bend there was a huge swamp. I suppose there was 100 acres in it, fed with undergrounds springs and water that drained into it from the fields. It was grown up in different kind of hardwoods and other trees. The coons and the possums stayed there during day time. Surrounding the swamp on one side was broom straw field where the rabbits lived. You could see the rabbit hawks flying over the straw field looking for rabbits and rats. I could imagine that all kind of things might be living in that swamp. You could walk in it during dry weather. But I did not venture very far into it.

Another activity I enjoyed on a few occasions was turtle hunting. After crops were laid by, no more plowing, and then harvest. There was a stream running behind our home and emptied into the river. We would go turtle hunting. Here is how we hunted turtles, the stream a few hundred yards before it emptied into the river had these large sand bars. The turtles I presume would come out of the river and bury themselves in these sand bars in the moist sand. You could see a yellow spot in the sand filled with water. We would take a stick with a nail in the end of it, with the head of the nail filed off, and push it down in the spot till it hit the turtle and then we dug it out, about six inches deep. These were mostly logger heads, and some soft shells. Their meat was delicious., cooked in lard in those days, after skinned and rolled in flour.

Whisky Still

Before Fred took over the land there was those that were engaged in producing moonshine whisky. John Henry Hardin was the king of all moonshiners. He was serving a prison term while we were living in the Bend. A few miles down the river from where we lived where no farming land was, there was an area that had thickets of bushes. He had hewn out a big clearing where he had his big still with dozens of still boxes where he fermented the mash. He had a huge boiler that produced the heat to distill the mash, producing the whisky. Much of the corn, or what ever he used, was boated across the river in a boat and likewise the whisky. When we visited the site the feds had come in and burst the boxes, and blew up the boiler with dynamite. I understand he bragged that he would die a millionaire or a pauper. I suppose he died as a pauper . After we moved from the bend across the Lovingood bridge into the brick home. More about the brick home later. He was out of prison and would come by our house on his way I guess to Canton in an old beat up pickup in low gear. We called him the mole because of his facial features like The Mole in Dick Tracy comics. His grandson became a good friend of mine and shared with me some of the things about his grandfather that were so sad.

River Fishing

Fishing was one thing we enjoyed in the Bend after the crops were laid by till harvest time. We fished with what you call trot lines. This consisted of stretching a line from one bank of the river to the other bank tying both ends to probably willow trees as close to the water as you could. Then we would weight it down with weights. We wanted it to be on the bottom of the river where catfish swim in search for food. We would take a rock and chip it where we could tie a cord around it and tie it to the trot line. . Then we would thread hooks on cords and tie them about three feet apart . Where we fished the river it was about fifty yards wide and very deep, and slow moving . It took a lot of hook lines to fill up a line . We most of the time we only had two of the trot lines in the water. One reason we had to go to some branch or creek and seine for minnows that we used for bait. We would do that during the day and bait the hooks before dark and then , as we called it, run the lines at night, or the next morning. We would do that about every hour or two all night. Maybe have two or three cat fish on each trot line. We had only two boats was one reason also that we did not put in more lines. I remember when we had built a camp fire close to the boat landing . We had arrived back at almost dark. This other fellow and I went to bait the hooks that were empty on one line. We took a long time getting back. When we got back to the landing they wanted to know what took us so long . It was dark then. I told them to shine their flash light in to the bottom of the boat. We had all kind of cats fish. We would tie the hook line to the trot line with a tie that all you had to do was pull the short string of the loop and it would come undone from the trotline and you did not have to worry about taking the hook out of the fish mouth. Then we would have a new line to replace the one that we had a fish on it. That same night the other fellows in their boat had been back from baiting their line. They would take off the dead minnows which was a mistake and replace it with a live minnow and did not throw some of the dead into the river. What we got our big hall on was dead minnows. When they started to get into their boat later to run their line, one of them shined his flash light down in the bottom of the boat and there was several snakes in the boat in search of those dead minnows, boy did they get a scare.

Dad like to fish for cat fish by tying hooks to branches that extended out over the water. We called these set hooks. I remember he had a bunch set out. He would always take someone to paddle the boat where he could tie the hook to the branch that would give if a catfish swallowed the minnow which floated or it swim till it died on top of the water It came a big rain and the river go up and when it went back down . To get his hooks, he took Paul Munday, a grown young man with him to paddle the boat. He would always tie the line with the loop knot and all he had to do was pull the short end and the line would come free. He told us, he was taking down all his set hooks and he came to one that was bent over, he though he had a fish on it but when he pulled on the line he thought maybe a log had caught on it when the river was up. So when he pulled hard on it, up came this huge catfish. I think it might have weighed 20 pounds. He said when he pulled it into the boat, Paul said," Great God what a fish." It was the biggest fish I had ever seen, a flat head yellow catfish My brother, who was almost six feet tall put its head at his waist, its tail turned up on the ground . We put it in our fish box in the branch and wanted to keep it alive. But I guess it had been out of the water too long and it died. When we saw it was dying, we skinned it and ate it. We gave some of it to Paul's family. But it wasn't all that tasty.

Mom would not let us shoot a gun on Sunday or on Christmas Day. One of the older Munday boys had joined the army and was shipped out to the Pacific, this was before Pearl Harbor. He could not tell where he was located for some reason. But the Christmas before he left he and his brothers, James and I, and some more neighbors went rabbit hunting on Christmas Day. We would jump a rabbit and surround it and catch it when it ran till it gave up. In his letter home he asked his family if they remember the rabbit hunt without guns. We then knew that he was stationed on Christmas Island in the Pacific.

THE SCARE OF MY LIFE

Before we leave the Bend, just a few more things come to my mind. The scare of my life. Paul Mundy and I had walked to the Lovingood bridge and met some young people to go possum hunting and on our was back of about a mile . The road that we traveled was a rough road that cars did not use, only wagons. At one point it ran right beside the river with a tall rocky bluff . I would say it was at least three hundred feet, almost strait up. Just about the time we were passing beneath the cliff, up on that cliff above us we heard this bone chilling scream. We described it, that it sounded like a woman screaming. You talk abut running. I know that 100 yard dash would have set an Olympic record. We then were out in an open sandy road in a field, out of breath. We were not the only person that had an encounter with was described as a panther . Levi Long and a friend , had stopped on the road that we used to walk to the one room school. Levi had got out of the car to use the bath room and went down in the woods a little way. All of a sudden he came running back to the car holding up his pants puffing and blowing the big cat had walked up on him . He said it was black and as large as a greyhound dog. There were hundreds of acres for it to roam in. Others had seen its tracks.

Syrup Mill

Dad was an expert in making syrup. Before we ever left Dawson county I worked at the syrup mill. My job was to thread the cane stalks through the rollers that squeezed out the juice into a wooden barrel cover with a burlap cloth to keep the yellow jackets out of the juice and strain the juice. It then ran through a pipe down hill from a wooden barrel to the cooking vat. The copper vat had different sections . the first would be the fresh juice, the second it began to heat, by the time it arrived at the last section it was boiling into some beautiful syrup. Wow, was it tasty. I would get me a cup, chew the end of a joint of cane and make me something to sop the hot syrup. Dad with a long handle stick with a square copper scoop fasten to it with holes in the bottom that would let the juice drip through it and would be dipping off the green skimming before it got to the last stage. The last stage had a spout where the syrup ran out into containers. It was stopped up with a tapered stick that was cloth covered to seal the spout until it was removed to let the syrup out of the vat. There was a lot of skill and experience to know when the syrup was done. Fire wood, some time slabs from the sawmills were used to fire the furnace that the vat set on , which was of rocks and mortar A mule turned the rollers that squeezed out the juice. There was a long tongue timber that was hewn out that was crooked enough that the end of it was almost on the ground and the mule was hitched to it and fasten to the tongue was a slim sapling that had a lead rope of a few feet that led the mule in a circle round and round. I sat on a wood block and a fed the cane stalks between the rollers. All the fodder had been striped off the stalks and the seed heads had been cut off. When I ran out of cane stalks I would go drag up new ones. Clean out the stalks already squeezed. The way the tongue was configured it would pass over my head and I did not have to duck my head when I was feeding it.

But the biggest operation that I ever saw at a syrup mill was in the Bend. Fred Willbanks brought in a gas generator and set up lights and the operation lasted night and day for several days as others helped . He and others hauled in truck loads of cane stalks. We had a large patch. James and I had to strip off the fodder and cut off the seed heads and haul the stalks to the mill. Dad did most of the cooking But it was worth it. Mom would heat the syrup for breakfast with some butter in it , cook biscuits and we had butter and syrup biscuits. Wow, that was good eating. And great to put in a paper sack to take to school for a meal, along with some sausage biscuits. No meals were served at school in those days.

One other thing before leaving the bend. I learned how to pan for gold. Mr.Mundy was a fox hunter, part time game warden and worked at saw mills. He had taught his boys and they taught me. Mr. Munday told of trying one night to sleep in this house. No one would live in it . The last person to lived in it was Paul Harding, son of John Henry the King of all bootleggers killed his whole family , five children, his wife and himself. He was about to go to prison , I guess for making liquor. Mr. Munday told of trying to sleep on the floor one night, when he heard this moaning , scared him so bad he took off. I went into the house once during the day. There were bullet holes all in the ceiling where this man had shot when he was drunk in bed. I killed a bobcat just a few yards from the house. The dogs had treed it. I shot it out of the tree.

Leaving The Bend Behind

As we crossed the river on the Lovingood Bridge. I bring you up the road for about a half of a mile to the brick house that I mentioned before where the Satterfields lived before they moved. The Blackstocks lived before you crossed the river. Ed, their son, was my age, he was my catcher when I pitched baseball in junior high.

The brick house was some more house. It was solid brick, not veneer. Plastered walls, the brick came from England. When ships sailed from England they were loaded with brick to weigh the ship down where it would not be bobbing in the water, then the ships would sail back to England loaded down with raw goods.

The brick home had four chimneys, eight fireplaces four down stairs and four upstairs. We never used any of the upstairs fire places, ten rooms if you counted the rooms where you climbed the stairs A full covered front porch the length of the house. What a shame that it was going to be destroyed before long. There was no indoor plumbing or electricity in the house. But a large barn for stock and cattle.

Back To The One Mule Farm

Before I write about living at Lovingood Bridge I want to take you back to the one mule farm in Dawson County. Life was simple and lot of fun on the one mule farm. Neighbors helped neighbors. I learned to pray early in life. Here is how it went. Mom had sent me to Effie Hamby's to borrow something she had need of to cook. She told me to go right there and back, and promised me a whipping if I did not. Well Cleon, Effie's boy my age, he and I started playing. One of our favorite activity was to find these wasp nest in the honeysuckle vines and rock them then we would run from the wasp. I forget what Mom had said. Then I remembered I ran as fast as I could run, praying every step of the way. Lord don't let Mama whip me. I guess He heard me and worked on Mama. She did not whip me or even scold me. I guess she expected me not to come strait back . I wonder if I thanked the Lord for answering my prayer. That happens today with adults, doesn't it?

Liberty School

I started to school at the two room school across the gravel highway from our house. In those days the first grade, they did not call it a grade , it was called primer . It was like kindergarten. Before you could go to second grade, certain thing you had to be able to do, like know your ABCs , count to one hundred, and be able to read the primer books. Well I could already do that. We had two sister teachers Erma Palmer and Pauline Palmer that rented our front bed room and boarded at our house. They taught me at home, before I was allowed to go to school. So I started to school in the second grade and graduated at 16 from the eleventh grade. We did not have twelve grades in those days. I learned a lot in that two room Liberty school. Different grades set in different rows facing the teacher and chalk black board . She or he would be teaching one grade while the other grades was suppose to be reading . But I would watch her diagram sentences and do arithmetic and I was way ahead of other students when we left Liberty to attend Lumpkin, where each class was in a separate room.

I can remember that Mom would have to get me out of bed. I guess I was maybe four. I would wait till she came and got me out of the bed, but one day one of the Palmer girls gave me a nickel to get out of the bed by myself. That did it, from then on I had to get myself out of the bed .

One of the funniest things Mom use to tell on me was this. The Palmer girls were getting ready to go to the school house . I walked into their bed room and they both had their hose on but they were standing there with them down around their ankles . And I put my hands over my eyes and told them to pull up their stockings.

Before I started to school I would slip across the road onto the red clay basketball court. It was packed down smooth from all the kids playing on it, with a back board on one pole, the hoop was home made by some blacksmith I guess, no net. They would leave the old laced up basketball out on the court and I would get it and try to get it up to the hoop. But could not, even when I took both hands down between my legs and try to throw it up. So after trying I would just wind up dribbling the ball. So I learned to dribble a basket ball pretty good even before I started to school. When I did get to go to school, I was the always the best dribbler on the team, even in junior high and senior high, and on other teams after high school.

THE TOY TRAIN

My children always expected me to tell this story in one of my Christmas sermons each Christmas. It happen when I guess I was maybe four years old. I don't remember if the Palmer sisters were still boarding with us or not. I am thinking they may have already moved somewhere else. It was time for the Christmas break , and the Palmer teachers had put up a Christmas tree in one of the rooms in the Liberty two room school house. It did not have any lights on it, there was no electricity in the school. But they had it all decorated with tinsels, popcorn stringed on thread, and wrapped gifts, They came to our home just across the road and took me to the celebration and the receiving of gifts from the teachers. There was one gift that stood out. It was a toy train about 10 inches long with wheels on it. No doubt everyone was wondering who would get that toy train. It was not wrapped. They began taking down the gifts and calling names of the boys and girls as they handed them out. But they waited to take down the toy train to be the last one. When they took it down they read my name. What a happy little boy I was. But that wasn't the greatest gift I ever received. My greatest gift was when I received the gift of eternal life. It wasn't a Christmas tree. It was the old rugged cross . Where Jesus shed His precious blood and purchased my redemption .

Possum Hunting

I don't know if possum hunting was my motivation or was it just to be with Dad on a one on one experience. He would be tired from working, but I would beg him for us to go possum hunting. I would say " Just a little while ." And finally he would give in and light up the old kerosene lantern . Once we walked out in the back yard and old Smitty saw us with the lit lantern, he would have a fit. He would take off and check out two persimmon trees near our house on the one mule farm to see if there were any possums in them or around. Then he would come back to us if he did not find one and off to the woods. He never barked until he had treed a possum. Except one night he treed. James and I were already in bed. Dad made us get up and go to him just a few yards from the house. It wasn't a possum, but rather a cat. He knew better, and when we got there he had his tail tucked between his legs, as we scolded him. That was the first and the last time he ever did that . He was a possum dog at night and a squirrel and rabbit dog in day time. When he treed a possum we could hear him and we would holler where he would know we were coming. When we got close enough we would say, "talk to him Smitty." He would really do some barking. We would shake the possum out if it was a small bush or we would have an ax and dad would cut it down. Sometimes I would climb the tree and shake it out. When it hit the ground old Smitty would grab it and it would sull up. As soon as we put the possum in the sack. He would take off hunting for another one. It would not be long until he had another one treed. The little while lasted for more than a little while. We would have to call him off of the hunt. Those were some great days that I like to remember.

Squrell And Rabbit Hunting

Old Smitty was a great squirrel dog. You could walk into the woods with him if you wanted to hunt squirrels, just start looking up in trees. He knew what you wanted. He would run a squirrel up a tree and then watch it to see if it jumped to another tree. You needed two to squirrel hunt, for the squirrel would hide on the opposite side of the tree. One could walk on the other side and shake a bush and the squirrel would go to the other side were you could see it and shoot it. I would go with Dad, and be the shaker. I could not at my age then shoot the shot gun.

We would take the squirrels home and skin them and if they were young squirrels Mom would fry them like chicken, but if they were older she would boil them and make squirrel dumplings.

Back in those days on the one mule farm and neighbor's property there were always an abundance of rabbits. No one posted their land. So I could put my rabbit boxes anywhere I wanted to put them, but tried to keep them close enough to our house that I could check them every morning before school. We also hunted them with dogs. I remember going on a rabbit hunt down in Forsyth country on Setting Down Creek. No telling how many rabbits bedded in the straw cover on one side of the creek. I think that there were four of five hunters, Dad, Uncle Henry and some more. I had become a good shot with a rifle. They would not let me go into the straw cover, but set me down on a stump on the outside in the field near the cover. And told me that I could shoot the rabbits when they ran out in the field. I don't think they expected this to happen. The dogs would jump a rabbit in the straw, they never got a shot, but there so many rabbits in there and they jumped so many different one, all they could see was the top of the straw moving and could not shoot. But I am seated out there on the stump and the rabbits would hop out in the field and stop, listing to the dogs bark. And I picked them off with my single shot rifle. When they came out I had a pile of them and they just walked by me as if they were not going to help me carry them They said , you shot them, you tote them. I remember I starting crying, and they came back and helped me. I did not realize that they were just joking to me. They were proud of my luck, down on their luck. Down on the creek behind Grandpa's house there were large Rabbits, twice the size of a cotton tail. We called them cane cutters, they ate canes in a cane thicket. I don't know where they came from, the only place I ever heard of any like them. They would bed down on the creek bank. If you jumped one it would jump into the creek which was shallow enough that they did not have to swim. We did not hunt them to eat.

Dad was the best of finding rabbits still in their beds ,and some distance from them . He said that he would see them back up ready to jump if we came close.

He would try to show me the rabbit in the bed. But I would look and look but just could not see it. He would jump it and as it ran off he would shoot it with the shot gun. If he shot it in the bed it would tear it up so bad that you did not have much left to eat. I remember one day I was hunting with my single shot rifle and I was trying to find a rabbit in its bed. But did not see it, till it jumped up and started up a path in the field and I shot it with the single shot 22 rifle and hit and killed it. I remember saying to the rabbit, " Yea, you thought you were going to get away" lucky shot.

More Liberty School

I have already mentioned the two room school house that we lived across the road from , the road was later paved with cement. The school had an upstairs to it, one big room. It was used in times past for a secret lodge. The Odd Fellows, but they did not meet any more. We were not permitted to go up there. They told us there was a goat up there. I got to go into it once, bunch of things that they used in their rituals . Had a coffin in there I think they put new members in it and then raised them to life. I guess they were imitating the resurrection of Christ. A poor example and heathen .

The school was heated with the old time pot belly stoves. The teacher would send us out in the woods behind the school. We would gather up dead limbs that had fallen in the woods and bring them for fire wood if the school ran low on cut wood. We would find some old rotten logs that had Bessie Bugs in them, a black bug, that looked like a 18 wheeler cab and trailer, about an inch long. We would gather us some of the bugs to chase the girls with.

Kids would bring their lunches from home and bring milk. There was a real cold spring back behind the school , about 40 yards I guess, maybe less. The school had a wire basket and the milk was put in the basket and lowered down in the spring to keep it from spoiling, If it was in the summer time.

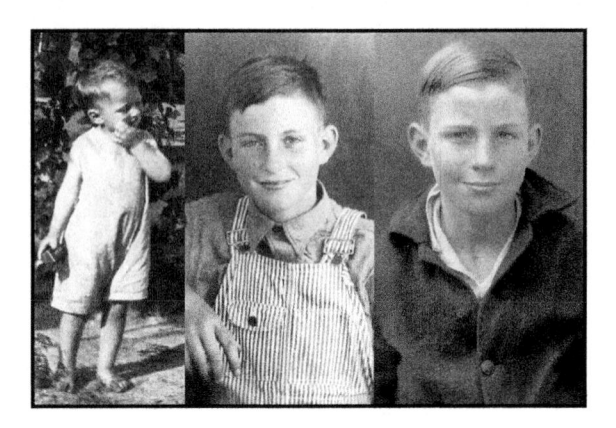

School Days Bill

Tornado Hits Gainesville

While we lived across from the school house before we moved to Cherokee county. I recall a lot of things about those days. I remember the morning of the devastation of the tornado that hit Gainesville. I recall as we walked out of the house that morning, the hot air hit us in the face. I can still hear Mom's voice even today, as she said coming from the garden, " There is going to be a bad storm somewhere today." She was right, in a short time after that the black clouds came roaring out of the South West. She gathered all the family and we went into the storm pit behind our house. It was dug back into a red clay bank with logs over it with dirt about two feet thick over the logs. And with a small entrance into the pit, with a door over the entrance. Fasten to posts imbedded in the ground and fasten to the logs above. We also had benches inside to sit on, it was about 12 x 10 feet and in one corner in the back of the pit a dug out hole that we would in the summer draw water from the well and fill up the hole to place the fresh milk which was warm to cool it for drinking and keep it from spoiling. Wow, corn bread and sweet milk, still is my favorite food.

We had a flood, lightening, rain and hail. Gainesville was 12 miles away by road. After the cloud passed and the sun came out, Henry , Dad's brother, and Grandpa Taylor pulled up in the yard. They had heard about the tornado on their battery radio. Hundreds were killed, many were trapped in a pants factory. The national guard was called in to the city to protect the property and to help recover the dead. I was able to go see the damage after several weeks. Dad , along with our citizens responded by going to Gainesville to help. I remember some of the things he told us that he observed.

Later after the city had rebuilt some of the city. President FDR came to dedicate a memorial for those that had died. I remember standing in the bed of a dump truck as he passed right under where I was standing He was making his way to where he was to speak, riding in his open limo with his cigarette holder in his mouth. The tornado was in the spring of 1936 I think. If it was, I was nine when it hit.

LIBERTY BAPTIST CHURCH

We lived close enough to the church that we walked to the church. I can remember Mom taking a quilt to church and placing it under the pew. The pews had a board on the front and back of the pew at the floor. She sat on the front pew and I would crawl under the pew, I guess I went to sleep. Later on I remember sitting beside her in the pew. I can remember some of her pinches when I was not sitting still and listening to the preacher. I also remember that some one would draw a bucket of water and place it on a stand near the pulpit for the preacher, or preachers, if there were others seated in the pulpit, visiting preachers in the congregation were always asked to come and fill the chairs in the pulpit. The bucket had a metal dipper with a long handle. I remember seeing children going up to the bucket and taking a dipper full of water, taking a sip then putting the dipper and water back in the bucket. Mom would not let me ever drink out of it. Wonder what the preachers thought about it. Guess they just stayed thirsty.

Got to tell you about this joke, don't know if it is true. But a friend told me this, it was passed to him from his mother. Back in those days, mothers breast fed their babies.

He said this woman was trying to get an older child to nurse, and he kept resisting her plea. The preacher was loud and fast and stopped to get his breath. When the woman was heard out loud say if you don't take it I am going to give it to the preacher.

We only had preaching on the second Saturday and Sunday. All business was conducted on Saturdays. The Clerk would read the minutes of the last Saturdays' meeting. An invitation was given during the business meeting for anyone who wanted to join the church. Also an offering was taken during the business meeting.

Sunday school was held every Sunday, and some times a singing in the afternoon and then the big meeting, revival, was held the second week in August, morning and night services. Since there was no electricity. Dad had the responsibility of preparing lights for the night services with lanterns, they were fueled with unleaded clear gasoline and air pumped into the bottom of the light where the gas was. The lantern had white mantels that would burn and put off a good light. When the light would begin to dim, you had to pump more air into the fuel tank to have more pressure.

I always looked forward to the second Sunday in May. They called it May Meeting, it was actually a home coming meeting with dinner on the grounds, (on tables outside) consisted in those days of planks laid across saw horses. Cover with table cloths. Do you know what I am talking about? Later on they bought smooth slabs from the Marble Hill quarries and built brick foundations for them to set on about three feet off of the ground. I looked forward to the good eating. You name it, it was there. One of my favorites were fresh cherries, strawberries, all kind of sweets. I would eat till I would almost pop. We pulled a good one on one of the older boys. Put some biscuits in his pockets, in his coat, and he did not know it, and when he was in a crowd , we asked him what he had in his pocket. We had a good laugh when he pulled them out.

Liberty Baptist School

Singing School

We did not have Bible School back in those days. In the summer we had singing school. It most of the time lasted for two weeks, Morning and Afternoon. Children and teen agers, sometime adults. We had to learn shape notes and sing the scale. Do, ra, me ---- And be able to recognize the shapes of the shape notes. We also had to lead songs and learn how to mark time with our hand. Down, right , left , up. If that was a certain timing for the song we were leading.

Uncle Ed Taylor conducted some of the schools and other singers, from Stamps Baxter's singers. Every year new books came out with some new songs, and we would learn the new ones as well sing some of those that were in books before. I remember one which was -TURN YOUR RADIO ON. Then there was another one. YOU WILL BE MY CLOSEITH NEIGHBOR UP THERE. I still remember a few words of each of these.

Dad led the singing in church services for maybe 60 years. He and Mom would sing a duet occasionally. He also was asked to lead the singing at other churches in revivals. Later on in my life if I went to a singing. If Uncle Ed was there, he would request that I lead a song. I would agree if he would play for me. One of those kind of singings was something. You would have dozens of people singing all four parts of a song. It was beautiful , the harmony.

Liightening Strikes

Back to the house across the highway from the two room, Liberty School. I guess I am blessed to be alive, and have lived all these years. It happen one morning when Betty and I were out in the back yard and Mom told me to go cover up a coop of little chickens under an oak tree some 50 feet from our house. I covered them up with some kind of tin and as I returned I was just fooling around. A cloud was coming up, not much of one. Mom hollered at us to get into the house, as she came from the garden above the house. Just as I took hold of the screen door, lightening struck that oak tree, killed all the chickens in the coop where I had been less than five minutes before. It shocked me so bad that I could not speak for a few moments and was still tingling a long time after, Betty also was shocked, not as bad as I was. The bolt also knocked a bucket out of mom's hand as she was coming from the garden some 200 feet from the tree on the other side of our house.

One of the funniest thing I ever saw happened at that same screen door. James and I were in the kitchen. I don't know what we were doing, but Mom was cooking. She grabbed a switch to use on us and we ran out of the kitchen , then out of the screen porch. Just as James hit the screen door a pig of maybe 100 pounds or more had got out of the pen and came and laid down right under the steps . And when he opened door and jumped out of the door the pig got up and he landed straddle of it. It started running strait up the bank behind the house with him on its back till he fell off backward. If that could have been captured on film it would be a winner.

Our house there was built on a slope. The back porch from the floor to the ground was just a foot or two off the ground the front of the house was about 6 feet. It had lattice from the floor to ground I suppose to keep the yard chickens and maybe the dogs from going under the house and also it made it more attractive. It had a door on the side of the house to enter under the house. That was where we put our sweet potatoes, and covered them with sand. If I got hungry, I would just go under the house and dig in the tater hill and get me a tater to eat. They would be cured and real good eating.

In that sand under the house dudle bugs, that is what we called them, don't know how to spell them, if there is one. They were about the size of a boa weevil. About the size of wood match head.. You could see where they had buried themselves in the sand about the size of a candy kiss turned upside down. You could get close over one of them and start saying dudle bug- dudle bug come out, and they would back out of the sand. Think we did not have anything to entertain ourselves in those days?

TRUCK WAGONS

We did not have tricycles, or bicycles in those days. But we did have truck wagons. They consisted of cutting wheels from a perfect round black gum tree, not sweet gum or any other tree. Black gum would not crack open when it dried out the other trees would. We wanted wheels for our back to be about 10 inches in diameter if possible and the two front wheels to be somewhat smaller. We would bore a large hole in the center of the wheels and make an axle out of a dogwood or hickory sapling . With a drawing knife cut the ends of the axle to insert through the holes. Then bore a small hole through the end of the axle and drive a stick in the hole to keep the wheels from coming off the axles, we would bore a hole in the center of the front axle after we had leveled it down for the seat plank to fasten to it with a bolt. The seat would be a plank with front end of it cut down to maybe six inches wide, were we could get our feet on the axle to guide it. The back of the board was nailed to the back axle and also had other boards cut at a angle to make the seat wider. Now you know how to make a truck wagon .Across the road and the branch we had a steep hill where we made our truck wagon road. We would drag our truck wagon to the top of the hill with a rope and down the hill we came, over and over again.

I would grease my truck wagon wheels with Mom's soap grease, I did not have any axle grease like what was used on a mule wagon. We had this dog that kept licking off the grease. So I came up with this bright idea, which worked. Mom had some red pepper drying on a string on the back porch. I decided to take some of it and put it on the grease to keep the dog from licking off the grease. I got the rough end of that experiment. I got that red pepper in my eyes and in my mouth. I ate about a pond of butter before Mom came to the house from the garden. And used a pan of water washing my eyes.

I guess by now you have noticed what I am writing has no chronically order. And probably a lot of errors . But I will get to the typographical errors later, just like to keep going as I think of other things.

I remember the first time that I spent the night with Grandpa Pa Grandma Taylor. I was so home sick, I wanted to go home. I sleep in the room with them. They had this clock , it was loud, tick tock , tick tock. Struck ever hour and dinged at the half hour. I liked to have never gone to asleep. When it got daylight I was all right.

Summer Time

I looked forward to summer time, when we lived across the road from the two room school house. Mom's nephew and my first cousin, Ralph Pharr, would come to see us. He lived in Barnesville

Georgia. He loved to fish and so did Dad. We would go to the Chestatee river to fish. I have been wondering how we got over there I guess Old Tob took us in our one horse wagon. Maybe Ralph came by bus from Barnesville. I remember one particular trip. Dad put me on his shoulder and waded the river to the middle of the river, gave me a cane and a can of worms and set me on a big flat rock to fish with a stringer to string my fish, if I caught any. I caught a string full of small channel cat fish. They were excited at my catch and so was I. They did not do as well as I did. Those cat fish coming out of that cold clear water stream, no pollution in those days, was a delicious meal. Mom cooked them for breakfast the next morning. I would guess.

Let us go back to Cherokee County for a while. We had moved into the large brick home that I have already written about. I was in junior high school when we moved. A lot of things to write about. It was about a half a mile down the hill to the flat bottoms to where you crossed Lovingood bridge to go down the river to the Bend where we lived before we moved. The Bridge was a one lane bridge spanning the river, I guess about 200 feet from one bank to the other. The Blackstocks lived on the other side of the bridge from us.

Our Two Dogs

We had two dogs, a German shepherd, Jack, and a Red bone hound, coon dog, Butler. We raised domanecker chickens in our yards. We began to see some white chickens in our yards. We were wondering where they were coming from. We just assumed that maybe some had escaped from trucks hauling chickens by our house. The road was just about 50 feet in front of our house between our house and the barn. One day Mom was in the kitchen cooking when she looked out the window and saw Jack coming up the road with a white chicken in his mouth. She watched him come to the back porch, which was like what we call a deck these days. Jack turned lose of the chicken and barked and the chicken flew off the deck. What had been happening before then was often Jack and Butler would dig up a ground hog out of its den in the sandy bottom. Jack would bring it to the back door and bark. Mom would open the door and there would be the dead groundhog. She would open the door and pat him on the head and give him some bread. He thought if he brought a chicken he was going to get fed. Instead he got a scolding. He did not try that again. We had to round up all the white chickens and take them back to the Blackstocks. How do you catch a yard chicken that is wild? Well take a fishing cane and tie to the end of it a wire, and make a loop like the loop in a metal close hanger, but smaller While the chicken is eating, maybe corn, slip the wire up and around the foot of the chicken and drag it to you as it can not get it's foot out of the wire loop as you pull it.

We had this mean old big red rooster that would run up behind Betty and flog her on her legs, scratching her legs. Mom remarked to me that she was going to kill that old rooster and cook it. The same time she had told me that I was going to the barn and he acted like he wanted to flog me. I picked up a wet corn cob and cut down on him. It hit him in the back of the head and killed him. I picked him up and took him to the back door. When she came to the door, I said, " Here is your rooster." She said, " I didn't mean today." Then I told her what happened. We ate that blessed thing. We did not sing that country song, " we will kill the old red rooster when she comes." We, or I, had already killed the old red rooster.

Catching Wild Hogs

Old Butler and Jack were two great dogs. Fred Willbanks had tried to raise some hogs in the Bend, it did not work, many of them got out and went wild. Some of them were big. He had told me and Gene Carlyle if we could catch any of these he would pay us for capturing them. I knew where some were across the river from where we lived. So Gene and I took Jack and Butler where they were and turned them loose after the hogs. One hog tried to swim the river where the water was shallow and Jack caught it in the middle on a big flat rock, He had it by the jaw and it was squealing . I waded out in the river, took this long rope and tied it to the hog and Gene had the end of the rope and he began to pull the hog toward the bank. Jack was biting its hind end. Once we got it out of the river with the help of Jack. We bent over a sapling and tied the rope to it where it would keep the rope tight where it could not get lose from the rope. We could hear another hog squealing . Butler had one caught. He could not bark, if he did he would have to let go of the hog, to let us know where he was, when the hog would quit squealing he would bite down hard on its jaw and it would squeal . He had captured this one down in a creek bed where it empted into the river in a thick mud bar. So I went down into the creek and tied another rope to this one and we drug it out and tied it up till Fred could come get them.

Fred's Bull, And Calves

Fred had some cattle in the pasture there at the barn across the road at the front of the brick home where we lived. He had this huge red Herford bull. He just had got himself through the old rusty wire fence and was over behind our house in the sweet potato patch eating on the vines. All I had to say was go get him Jack. He took off and grab that bull by the nose and threw it down. You never heard such bawling as it lay there on the ground flat of his back. When I called off Jack, that bull took off toward the barn and the pasture. He did not stop to stick his head through the wire as he did when he got out he hit that wire fence full speed and broke the old rotten wire, because Jack was biting on his heals.

Fred also had some breeder beef cows in the pasture an the calves they had birthed that was getting to be good size. The whole herd of calves got pink eyes and we had to put medicine in their eyes. James, my brother who was four years older than me would grab one by its ears and try to wrestle it to the ground for me to put the medicine in its eyes. It would drag him all over the lot before he would finally get it on the ground. But I had a better idea. I would take my thumb and index fingers and catch them in their nostrils and with my nails biting into their tender nose and twist, they would fall on their sides, and he then would put the drops in their eyes.

Did you know that you can scratch a hog on it's side and it will lie down and let you keep scratching it?

Comic Books

Let us go back to my childhood at the one mule farm where we lived on the highway from Gainesville to Dawsonville, in Dawson county. I enjoyed reading comic books, we called them funnies. Gulf Oil Company used to print a comic book, it came out ever so often. The main character in the book was Smiling Jack he was an aviator. And there was also Little Orphan Annie and Sandy her dog, Daddy Warbucks the rich man and Punjab the giant . And the stories were always written that you could hardly

wait to read the next edition .We would watch for those orange colored Gulf trucks to come by our house and we would run to the road and holler, " Throw us some funnies." The driver would throws us some out. He was delivering oil to Gulf stations. Because of those free comics, when I needed gas later in life, and had a choice, I always bought Gulf. That gift to a child , paid great dividends for the gas company.

I also liked Dick Tracy, Popeye and Olive, we did not get a paper, but Emmitt Warren our neighbor did and we would get funnies from him. I also borrowed novels from neighbors. I liked Zane Gray's writing, my favorite novels was RIDERS OF THE PURPLE SAGE and BLACK BEAUTY.

Our mail route was Star Route. Gainesville Georgia. Our mail carrier carried the bag of mail from Gainesville to Dawsonville and he delivered personal mail to everyone on the highway. He was very helpful . If Mom did not have a stamp, she would put her letter in a clothes pin and put three pennies with it clamped to the letter. He would put a stamp on the letter. He also delivered a bag of mail to our neighbor Emmet Warren, who was a rural mail carrier. He carried me on his mail route on one occasion before I started to school. He always stopped at a store in Silver City, a wide place in the road, on highway 9 between Cumming and Dawsonville and bought a Coke-a- Cola . And he bought me one to drink. I had never drank from a bottle, so I turned it up and I guess I put the bottle in my mouth and took a big swig and then belched and it came out my nose, set me on fire and I began to cry, he laughed at me , then showed me how to drink from a bottle. Did you know that a Coke Cola had cocaine in it until 1903 . People call it dope. My Dad if we went into a store would often say do you want a dope. In cotton mills they had a dope wagon that came through the mill. I understand they still called it the dope wagon even after other drinks were available from it.

A Barb Wire Fence

Before we sold the ONE MULE FARM, we had a pasture where we kept our milch cows , that is the right way to spell milch, it is an adjective , not a noun. Our milch barn was there. Mom had let me go barefooted that eventful day. I was so glad to get off those heavy brogan shoes. Thought that I could jump over the moon. I took off across the pasture toward the road where Uncle Henry Taylor built his house after he bought the farm from Dad. I was going to jump the fence, and just before I tried to jump it, it came to my mind that I was going to land in a hard road bed. There was a bank there before Henry leveled it to build his house. So I tried to stop and fell over the fence. I still carry a six inch scar on my left calf. The barb on the fence cut an inch deep slash down my leg . It bled very little , since it was fatty flesh. Dad took me to Dawsonville to Dr. Palmer, he cleaned out the cut and bandaged it up with gauze and tape. He said it was too deep to sew up it needed to heal from the inside first. It took it over a year to heal.

For you that go by Uncle Henry and Aunt Lillian's house and make your way to Liberty Baptist Church, if they are still uncut, you will see a stand of pines which I planted in 1942 as a FHA project the year that I went to high school at Dawsonville High. I was staying with Grandpa and Grandma Taylor. I went my senior year to Acworth High School, and boarded in a boarding house. I worked for a five and dime store part time to pay for my board. We loaded products from the warehouse to a truck to be carried to their other stores. Those of us that worked there had plenty of peanuts to eat, we would open one of the boxes of peanuts then leave it on the shelf and help ourselves to them.

Lovingood Bridge

You will notice that my writings are not in any chronically order if it makes any difference to you. So let me take you back to where we lived at Lovingood bridge. The river one winter froze over solid, bank to bank. James walked out on the ice, scared me. I though for sure it was going to break and he would fall in, at my begging he got off the ice. Then he and I got a huge rock all we could do to get it up on the bridge. And we pushed it off, thinking it would break the ice, it only made a white place and skidded .It was during that time that we had the biggest snow I have seen in my life time. Had one big snow, and the snow did not melt and then it came another one about a week later. Did not bother us, didn't have any power that could go off. Plenty of fire wood, kitchen stove wood, and indoor plumbing , chambers, no pipes to freeze. And a well full of. water and a couple of cows in the barn. Wasn't going anywhere. So we just sit before the fire place . The brick house was easy to heat. We would pop popcorn and we would make some popcorn balls. We did that by cooking syrup till it would ,when cooled, be sticky and hard. Stir it into the popcorn , wash our hands ,and grease them with butter to keep the syrup from sticking to our hands as we balled up the corn into balls. We had a home made corn popper that we would stick over coals in the fire place. It consisted of what was called a whisky can. Dad would take a can cutter and cut down the top side of the can , fasten it to handle, maybe a mop handle , bend back the cut top of the can that when you pushed it back down there would be tension on it and then place a nail through the front that would hold down the lid. And he would make nail holes all over the can. As we held it over the coals we would shake it . He would have cut out the back of the can and cut a piece of a plank to be the back part of the popper, and bored a hole in the wood to insert the handle a broom or mop handle, great popper, just as good as the wire poppers and holding more corn. We had a saying when the popcorn started popping, " Lindsey Lowe is coming". Back in Dawson County, it seemed like every time we popped corn he would show up at our house for a visit about the time it started popping. By the way we grew our own popcorn.

So we survived those cold winter nights, I suppose, I am still here. But summer was my favorite time, since the river was so close for swimming. About an every day a skinny dip. We had a boat, home made, flat bottom, twelve inch side board planks. Bent in the front for it being more narrow in front. To plow through the water as we paddle it across the river where we had some grape vines and we would swing on one that we had cut and act like Tarzan and drop into the water, that was fun. I also like to fish and there was plenty of cat fish in the river. Mom would not let me fish on Sunday, but one Sunday, Gene Carlyle and I slipped off to the river and put out some set hooks, which consisted of taking some canes with sharp ends , where you could stick them into the banks at an angle then a fish could nor pull out the cane. It would just bend when the fish pulled on the hook and line. It came up a cloud burst that afternoon . Catfish will feed after a rain . Gene and I slipped off to the river to run our set hooks. We had already caught two or three smaller fish, but when we got to the last cane, it was bend way over, we knew we had a big one. I pulled the cane out of the bank and when I tried to pull it up the bank. Gene was trying to get his hand in it gills. He said it bit him. I told him to hold the cane and I would get hold of it. I did but my feet slipped and I slid into the river with it. It was only about waist deep. I held on to the fish and Gene helped pull me out of the river with the cane That one weighed about nine pounds, a blue cat. We were so excited we had to take the rebuke from Mom for fishing on Sunday. But we were so excited that we had to show off our catch, and we took the fish and put them in our fish box in the branch near our house. We sold them to someone from Canton who would often come by our house and ask if we had any fish.

I pulled a good one on James my brother while we lived there. He and I both were still in junior high, he had to drop out of school for two years because of Dad's health. We were aboard our wagon with a team of horses going down the hill toward the bridge on our way to cross the bridge and get a load of wood that we had cut. The bed of the wagon had been removed and what we were riding on was the running gear of the wagon. I had found a dead rabbit and I stuck it up under the lip of a bank, were we sometimes would see a live rabbit. So as we passed by he was looking for a live rabbit when he spots the dead rabbit, of course he did not know it was dead. When he saw it he stopped the horses , jumped off the wagon and ran to the house to get Dad's shot gun. I pulled the wagon a little further away where the horses would not be scared at the shooting of the gun. He takes aim and shoots at the rabbit, it did not move and then he shoots again. I hollered and told him he had missed it and started laughing. By that time he knew he had been had. He fussed at me for making him use two of his shells, but we had a big laugh about it and so did Mom and Dad, and I guess Betty, my sister.

COTTON TO CHICKENS

We planted 12 acres of cotton behind the brick house, you have never seen such cotton stalks. We made over 12 bales of cotton on those acres. It took it a long time to open, didn't all open to after frost and the leaves fell off of the stalks. But Dad decided that he was through raising cotton and was going to start raising chickens. Preacher Gazaway, pastor of Liberty back in Dawson county, who lived in Cumming was in the chicken business. And he agreed to furnish the baby chicken for Dad. So Dad built two chicken houses out of lumber he had torn from some abandoned houses across the river. While he was building the two houses, he received a hatching of baby chicken and we put them in an old house up the road from where we lived, about I guess fifty yards. He and I were spending the first night with them and seeing that the heat was right and that they did not pile up and smother each other. We were sleeping on some quilts spread on the shavings. Suddenly he begin to scream. I did not know what was going on, but a wheat bug had crawled down in his ear and was biting him in his ear. Ever time it bit he would holler. We took off to the house and Mom poured some warm water in his ear and the bug crawled out. But Dad refused to go back , but I went back and spent the night with biddies.

Once he had finished the first house, with a dirt floor. He ordered a batch of biddies. The brooders were made out of 60 gallon drums. We fired then with green pine wood, it did not burn fast. In those days it took 12 weeks to raise a broiler to two and a half pounds . I don't think it was the first flock we raised. But one in the first house he built. The curtains were open and a stray dog raised up and looked into the window and scared the chickens and they piled up on each other and about a hundred smothered and they were ready for market. So we started gathering up the smothered chickens, which were still warm, pulled off their heads to let them bleed and skinned chickens for hours. You don't pick feathers off a hot house chicken that you get from a chicken house, you skin it. When we had finished all of them, Dad took them to Canton to a freezer locker We had a lot of chicken to eat for a long time. Remember we did not have electricity.

The old house where Dad got the bug in his ear it had a front porch on it. A tin room on the house behind the front porch. I slept upstairs in the brick house and my window was facing the old house. I had the window up, no screen on it, and I heard some one talking. It was a moon light night, and I could see a couple of guys standing eating watermelons on the edge of the porch. Dad had a patch just across the road. I decided I would have me some fun. I had my automatic 22 rifle in my room. I rested it on the window cell and started shooting into the tin roof. You talking about making tracks they did up the road. I knew who they were. Dad would not have cared for them helping themselves to the watermelons. He was an expert in raising melons. He would have us plow a deep furor and filled it in the fall with compost, later chicken manure, and let it lay there over the winter, and when time came to plant the seed he or we, would cover up the manure. Then make a bed from each furor and plant the melon seed. When they started putting on small melons he would put a pinch of soda, nitrogen, fertilizer close to the vine roots. He always thinned the plants to two per hill. He raised some huge melons. He had bought and old chivy car that had been made into a pick up, with a wood bed on it, and while we lived there he would load up that old pick up with melons , place some straw or hay in the bed to keep them from rolling around in the bed. He then would take them to Canton, and stop at small stores, and the store owners would buy a few to sell. It did not take him long until he had sold his load.

That old pick up was the first car that our family owned since I could ever remember . It was the first one I tried to drive. It had a lot of loose play in the steering wheel and I had a hard time keeping it between the ditches till I got some experience. But I learned to drive it, and when I went to Cartersville to get my driver licenses. The examiner asked me how long I had been driving , when I told him how long, he did not give me a driver test.

BASEBALL

I guess my years as a baseball player probably began while we lived at Lovingood Bridge. Although at the two room school house where we lived in Dawson county. We played what was called Town Ball, don't know where it got the name. It consisted of a soft rubber ball about the same size as a baseball, it was solid soft rubber, I remember that it was red. We batted with flat bats, made from a board and trimmed down for a handle, like a paddle for a boat, not for your butt. The batter would strike the ball and those in the field would try to catch it on the fly or first bounce for an out. If someone was on base and the ball was hit to an infielder and they did nor catch the ball for and out they could throw the ball at the runner and if they hit a runner, that runner was out. No base stealing I remember that I came down with mumps on the last day of school and had not missed a day. George Townsend came over to the house and told Mom to send me on to school. He told her he had several there with the mumps. Mom agreed and told me no playing ball, but I could not resist the temptation.

But while living at Lovingood Bridge we did not play Town Ball we played baseball. Our ball a lot of times was a base ball that had lost its cover and we had wrapped it in back rubber tape. We played pasture ball. I did most of the pitching. We did not have gloves, we caught the ball bare handed. The batter which was batting had been the hind catcher before he came to bat. He would stand some distance behind the batter and field the ball that the batter missed or did not strike at and throw it back to me as the pitcher , or another pitcher. But we had a team at New Bethel, and I was the pitcher, we had gloves and a regular baseball. Ed Blackstock was my catcher. It was a rocky field and second base was a huge flint rock. We were not allowed to steal a base of slide into a base, could run by it and not be tagged out.

I remember playing against another school, Sixes school. What I remember most about that game ,which we won. James my brother came to the plate with a softball bat rather than a baseball bat, and hit a ball almost out of sight for a home run. I guess there was no rule that he had to use a baseball bat.

I remember we also played against Woodstock, these were Junior High Schools. I did not get to play any baseball after I finished junior high, when I attended Dawsonville High and stayed with Grandma and Grandpa . Dawsonville did not have a baseball or basketball team Their gym had burned and they had not fielded a baseball team before then at anytime. But I kept my arm in shape. Grandpa had an old store building with a real thick door . I guess for security reason. There was a pine knot showing in the door about waist high. I would back off about the distance from the door as it was from the mound to the plate. I would throw, and pick up the ball as it bounced back toward me and walk back to my mark and throw again. I heard Grandpa talking to Grandma one day about someone trying to break into his store house. I was bursting the door. I got me a rubber ball and I would throw it and field it as it came off the door. When I transferred to Acworth for my senior year. I got to play baseball again, but I did not pitch. I played third base and was one of the leading hitters on the team. I was invited by the Atlanta Crackers to come to Atlanta for a tryout once I finished high school. But I did not go. I went to work the next day after I graduated at Bell Aircraft in Marietta. Played in a few games with the plant team. I was just sixteen, became seventeen in August.

Bill and Baseball

PEARL HARBOR

It was Sunday, December 7,1941. I was 14 at that time. Dad, James, my brother, and I had gone that Sunday afternoon to a farm that Fred Willbanks farmed where there were loads of walnuts off of the trees on the ground. We had picked up several sacks full and brought them back to our home at Lovingood Bridge. Looking forward to Mom cooking some walnut cakes. When we drove up into the yard, Mom came out of the house and told us that the Japanese had bombed Pearl Harbor. She had been listen to our battery radio. I remember saying, " Who do they think they are? We will blast them off the map in no time." How wrong I was, we did blast them, but it took the A-Bomb to finish them off. As a side note I was in Pearl Harbor a few months after the surrender of the Japanese . As my ship entered Pearl , the smell of diesel fuel from the sunken ships still seeping into the harbor was so strong floating on the water. Ever time I smell raw diesel fuel, I get a flash back. I was stationed there for a while and had to go to Pearl often to pick up USO personnel arriving. I had been assigned as a chauffer for Fleet Entertainment. Our group of sailors lived off the base , about 10 of us in a USO barracks , an Army barracks, Ft Derussey for rest and recovery on Waikiki Beach. I observed while station there many of the bomb craters that occurred during the attacks, at Hickman field and Schofield Barracks.

My sister Betty, tells me that on Monday after the attack that Glynn Hubbard, the Principal at New Bethel JR High, brought all the students into the assembly room, and let us listen to our President, FDR, as he declared war on Japan. Mr. Hubbard had brought his radio to the school. I don't remember him doing that. I just remember the broadcast of the speech. Let us not forget Pearl Harbor. I may have worked on the B-29 that dropped one of the A-Bombs. As I have already mentioned that the day after I graduated from high school at 16 I found my self up in the engines of the B-29s removing the carburetors , taking them to machine shop of the plant where they drilled a hole in them an installed a thermo bulb in them to be able to fly the planes higher and icing would not occur in the fuel. That was what we were told. These planes were not made in Marietta, but in St. Louis by Boeing and flown to us for us to modify them. Once we had them all modified, I started working on Bell built planes. Wonder how I got a job with Bell as a sixteen year old person? Well I did not have a birth certificate to show them , my class mate and good friend, Bobby Cantrell, signed an affidavit that I was seventeen.

Bill in the Navy

ON THE WAY HOME FROM CHURCH

The big meeting was a special time at Liberty Baptist Church. It was the second week in August, morning and night services. With Baptismal service for those saved on the third Sunday. It was a time of gathering at Grandpa and Grandma's house . Grandkids and others. We walked to church from their house and back, even at night. I recall that one night a crowd of relatives were walking back and when they were about a hundred yards from the house. Old Jack, a black dog, came up the road to meet us. I was back behind the people and when he came to me I pulled off my white shirt and tied it around it and took a stick like I was going to whip him and told him to go home. It was dark that night, and when he passed the folks up front he went up in the field to pass them and all they could see was that white shirt going by, Scared the daylight out of some of them. They were screaming, boy did I have a laugh out of that prank.

But there was another prank that backfired on me and Ben Hulsey. Which we kept it as our secret. Ben is my third cousin. He was spending the night with me at Grandpa Taylor's. We were fooling around behind my brother, Lillian and Henry, and maybe someone else. Just up the road from where Henry built their house was a steep hill before it was cut down to be paved. One of those quick and up over that takes your breath if you was going fast in a car. The road scrape had scraped the road and pulled a lot of loose dirt out into the road. We had heard that there was a certain fellow from another community would be coming up that way on his bicycle. We figured he would be pushing it up that hill. So we get this bright idea to pull a trick on him. There was a lose telephone wire hanging from a telephone post from what was a community telephone line that had been abandoned. So we pull the wire across the road and tied it to a pine bush on the other side of the road. About the time we got it tied, here comes this car running fast. We started trying to get the wire untied. But could not get it untied in time . The car ran into the wire and it pulled the wire loose from the pine bush and where it hit the car was right under its headlights . In those days there were exposed light wires and it tore them out and they went about fifty yards before they got stopped. And they had to leave their car. Ben and I took off to the woods and stayed there till we saw them leave the car and walking up the road .I would whistle to him and he back to me then we went on to Grandpa's . Were late getting there, scared to death. Did not go into where James and the rest of the folks were. We went to bed. We heard James say, it sounded to me like the high gear stripped in the car. Ben and I pledged to each other we would never tell anyone about that crazy act.

Years later after we both had married. He and his wife came to see Eva and me in Cumming. I asked him if he had ever told anyone about that crazy act. So we told our wives about it. Now the secret is out in print, and the driver of that car will not be around to have us thrown in jail.

Bill and his brother Robert

UNCLE BILL JENKINS

There was one character in the Liberty community that was a real character. Everyone called him Uncle Bill, even though he was not their uncle. He was scared to ride in a car. He walked everywhere he went, and he walked in a lope, fast, he would walk all the way to Gainesville. I bet that he walked it in two hours. He was a slim skinny person, no wonder. Gainesville was twelve miles away. People would offer him a ride but he would not accept it. He did one day accept a ride. I can't mock his talk in print.

It was funny. He was looking worried and the driver asked him if he was scared and he said. "I am worried that we might meet another fool driver like you."

One night in the summer time we were out in our back yard and we heard a car crash down below the church on the highway. Uncle Bill thought his wife was in the car. She was over at their son's house and he had seen the headlights come down the road to the highway. We heard him screaming all the way to our house almost a mile away. But Lidia, his wife, was not in the car. It was a neighbor. He had run into the cement creek bridge rail post. He had had a few drinks to many. We use to say that yodeling was invented by Uncle Bill as he would holler O Lidia.

Preacher Gazaway use to tell on Uncle Bill this story. He was baptizing a group in a pond in a pasture . Uncle Bill was saved and was being baptized . In those days those that we being baptized would hold hands and walk out into the water, with the pastor at the head of the line. I don't know what was going on that day. About the time he was going to baptize Uncle Bill, in that sort of horse voice, said, " Great God what a snake." He had spotted it in the water somewhere. He lived to be quite an old man. When in later years and I would be at Liberty Church for a Sunday. He would come up to Dad and ask him if I was going to preach. He would say if he ant I am going home.

CHRISTMAS FUN

One of the things that I enjoyed at Christmas was going serenading. We would have a large bunch of young people, kids and a few adults. We would dress up in some kind of disguise. Masks, stockings over our faces with holes in them for our mouth, nose, and eyes with lip stick paint, like an Indian, water color paint. Men with dresses on, all kinds of costumes. We would approach a house and slip up quietly on the front porch, most of the houses had front porches in those days, where people sat in hot days and late at night when it was awful hot till the night cooled down. Then we would start ringing cow bells, beating tin pans, and hollering. When the occupants open the door we would pile into the house and the neighbors would try to identify each of us. A lot of folks were expecting us some time or another and had something to give us to eat if we wanted it. I remember on one occasion when we went to this house that the folks had a mean little dog. George Pugh was wearing a dress and that dog got hold of the dress and George was going round and round trying to dislodge the dog which was holding on and swinging in the air.

We did not pull any of the pranks that Dad used to tell us that they did when they were young. They would go to a neighbor's barn and get his cow and take it to another neighbor's barn and exchange it for his mule and take the mule back and put it where the cow supposed to be. When the neighbor came out to milk there was the mule. And when the neighbor went to feed his mule there was the cow.

Mr. Lawernce Towsend's Store

His store was our closest store about mile from our home down the highway toward Gainesville. That is where we would go to buy those thing Mom needed for cooking and kerosene for our lamps. He would accept eggs for what we bought if we did not have the cash. That was were I took my rabbits that I had caught in my rabbit boxes and he would give me cash for them, and most of that was spent on candy. He sold the rabbits to what was called a barter man . If I was buying something for Mom and not for myself. He would always give children a few of the candy chocolate   kisses . I looked forward to going to the store,

I can remember he had a gasoline pump in front of the store. Since he had no electricity at the store. The gasoline had to be hand pumped up into a glass container on the top which had on the outside of marked the number of gallons that you had pumped. There was long wood handle on the side of the pump and you would move it back and forth and the gas would flow down into the glass tank.

I remember one day at Liberty School I saw the first air plane that I had ever seen in person, might have seen one high in the sky, don't remember if I had. We heard this plane circling our school real low. The teachers let us all run outside to see the plane. It was a bi- plane, that meant it had two wings, and open cockpit . The pilot was waving at us as he circled. Mr. Townsend's hose to his gas pump had developed a leak and the pilot had brought him a new one, circling real low over the store and dropped it out of the plane.

When all of us were back in our class rooms. We were all excited. Mr. George, our teacher talked about air travel. He told us that some day a person would be able to eat breakfast in Georgia and supper in California. I started thinking about in my child mind. I remembered being in the Gallant-Belk store in Gainesville and buying something. You did not pay for it at a cash register, the clerk would make out a sales slip, she would put it in a cup and a vacuum would zip it upstairs to an office and just in a few seconds, down would come any change you were due and your receipt. They now have these at drive through banking. I visualized that they would build a large one like that to take passengers to different cities. There has been research on such. But with advancement of aviation, it is possible to leave North Carolina at breakfast and get to California before you left, according to the clock.

Sanky Hughes Store And Mill

About two mile from us toward Dawsonville was Sanky Hughes' store and corn mill. That was where we took our shucked corn to be ground into meal. It consisted of two granite round stones that set on top of each other that turned and ground the meal. He had a lever that adjusted the distance between the stones. I would watch him feel of the meal as it pored out into a container to test the thickness of the ground meal. He would take our ears of corn and place them in a corn sheller that ran on a belt from a car motor that also had a wide belt that turned the stones. When the corn came out of the sheller, he would take a scoop and scoop a couple of scoops which was his charge for grinding the corn. I can see that old car engine that he used for the power. For the radiator, he had a 60 gallon barrel full of water and the hose pipes running down into the barrel. I remember the sound of that motor when he cranked it. It did not have a muffler on it. So no use trying to talk over that sound. He carried a lot more in his store than Mr. Townsend, of that which farmers needed. There is on highway 400 where the Gainesville and Dawsonville highway crosses 400 there is a store called Sanky's Place. His son, Horace, married my beautiful first cousin, Gladys Bennett.

Lumping School

Liberty School was closed and I started attending Lumpkin elementary school , when a student graduated from Lumping , they attended Dawsonville. I received my first whipping in school their. Another student cut my initials on the top of my desk. When the teacher saw it she whipped me with a switch. I did not feel it. I had on lace up boots that covered the calves of my legs. I remember I cried, my feeling were hurt. I receive a whipping that I did not deserve, because I was innocent.

I had a crush on a girl at Lumpkin. She was Maxine Bruce. She lived right close to the school. She wore some real pretty dresses. I don't think she had a crush on me. But we were friends. She looked like Shirley Temple. She had a brother killed in World War 2. She went on to become a teacher. Her Dad and Mom were members of Liberty Baptist Church.

I had my first experience as an actor at Lumpkin school. I don't remember the name of the play All I remember is that I was the main actor. I loved being in the play.

This reminds me of a couple of plays that I had a part in at New Bethel. I remember those. One was, Aunt Samantha Rules the Roost. The other was, Aaron Slick from Pumpkin Creek (Pronounced – Crick) . I think I was Aaron Slick, and in the other one I was the handy black man around the home and Begonia was the black maid and cook . I was in the kitchen trying to steal a kiss from her and accidently turned over a pot of flowers and spilled water all over the table. This wasn't in the play. But the audience did not know it. I am trying to put the flowers back in the pot she was hitting me over the head with towel and we were adlibbing. The audience was rolling with laughter. The cast behind the screen was able to see what was going on for quite a while and splitting with laughter. When the curtain closed for the next act, and we went behind the stage they were still laughing.

Dawsonville High School

When I graduated from New Bethel Junior High. I went to live with Grandpa and Grandma Taylor, and helped Henry and Lillian in the chicken houses built at my grand parents. I was in the tenth grade, only had 11 grades in those days.

I had some good times that year. Beulah Woods, got me a nick name. She sorta liked me and I did her, and picked at her on the bus. And she would say you old buzzard leave me alone. Wasn't long till about everyone was calling me Buzzard.

I remember , Silvia Robertson was the bus owner and the driver of the bus. Bus routes were contracted to owners of buses. Leon Robinson, a nephew of his, was in the back of the bus and threw a rotten apple at me and I ducked and it whizzed by Silvia and splattered on the Windshield just missing him. Well both of us were not going to be allowed to ride the bus. Grandpa had to go to talk to the County School Superintendent to get me back on the bus.

We had one teacher at Dawsonville High we called Old Glory, not where she could hear us. The reason , she had dyed hair that was red, white and blue. It wasn't a fad in those days, she just did not do a good job dying her hair. She was from Virginia and had that Virginia accent, that we laughed at.

While attending Dawsonville High and living with my grand parents. Ray Clarence Bennett, a nephew of Grandma, also lived with them. I remember he had a model A coup. He, I, and three of the Robinson boys, Leon and his two brothers, we had a string band and we would go around to older peoples' homes and play and sing hillbilly music and songs for them. They would most of the time have something to offer us to eat. Ray Clarence's coup had a rumble seat which some of us had to ride back there in the outside of the front seat. I remember one time when it was raining all five of us were in the front seat, sitting in each other's laps. I was sitting in Ray Clarence's lap steering the car, he was mashing the gas and the brakes and we were going so fast that I cold not make the turn of the curve and ran up on the bank before he got us stopped. Our musical instruments were in the rumble seat in the back closed.

Uncles

These are uncles who were Grandpa Taylor's sons or married one of his daughters. Dad was the oldest of the sons.

Uncle Ed was after him. I did not spend a lot of time with him until I was older and when we moved back to Dawson County. I saw him more at church and at singing.

Uncle Ray was next. He had suggested that I come to Cumming Georgia and open a barber shop. I had graduated from Barber College in Atlanta and was barbering in the Dixie Hunt Hotel Arcade in Gainesville with five other barbers. So I set up to barber in Cumming and also opened a beauty shop in the same building. When Eva and I got married Dec. 24, 1948 we set up housekeeping in an apartment upstairs over Dr. Howell's Dentist office. I got to know uncle Ray and aunt Corrine. Bobby who worked next door in the drug store. Also Marjorie their daughter, who was in school . She was eight or nine I guess when we were married. Our oldest daughter, Diane, was born in Cumming.

Uncle Henry was next. He was more like an older brother. I never addressed him as uncle. It was Henry and Lillian. Betty and I would go and spend the night with them when they lived up on the hill in the renter's house. He would turn the lights on from his car and we would shoot marbles. He wasn't much of a shot and I was . I would win his marbles and then he would buy them back and we would go at it again. There was no electricity in the house, or any in the community.

Bill's Uncles, Henry, Ray, Ed and Bill's Mother and Father

UNCLES THAT MARRIED GRANDMA AND GRANDPA'S DAUGHTERS

I guess that Uncle Kiel Bennett was the oldest of those Uncles. Since he married Grandpa and Grandma's oldest daughter, Nora. I remember him sitting on the front porch at Grandpa and

Grandma's smoking a cigar and he had a laugh that I loved to hear.

Then there was Uncle Anderson Whidby that married Aunt Onie. I did not know him much when I was young, but got to know him better after I was a preacher and his third wife had died.

Then Uncle Joe Carruth , who married Aunt Bertie . I guess I knew him the best. I can remember visiting them when Joe Jr was small, when they lived in Forsyth County. I remember the lake , He , Dad and others built . Using a mule to pull a bucket scrape , and when they got to where they wanted to dump the dirt. They would lift the handles turn it over and then with the scoop upside down , the mule would pull it back for another bucked full of red clay dirt.

But I got to know Uncle Joe , later in life, and a few times slept in the same room with him at Grandpa's. I didn't sleep much. He could snore louder than anyone I ever heard. After I answered the call to preach, I had an opportunity to talk to him concerning his relationship with the Lord. It was a happy day when I heard he had made a profession of faith and had joined the Methodist church with Aunt Bertie. I remember preaching at Liberty Church and after the services he came up to me and told me that he had heard three sermons already that day. One early at the lake, then his church and then me at Liberty. My mother told me that he told her that Billy is going to pastor a large church someday, which I did, more than just one.

Uncle Hoke Parks , He and Aunt Mamie Bell came to visit Grandpa and Grandma Taylor, with their children often , before we moved to Cherokee county, and Dad had sold the One Mule Farm. He was a card. He liked to pick at kids. I remember he could wiggle his ears. I also remember he could pinch you with his toes. He taught me how to feed the crow. He would cross his fingers and when you put your finger down between his four fingers he would pinch it with his thumb. One time is all that it took for me to wise up to that.

My Grand Parents On My Mothers'side Of The Family

I never knew my Grand Parents on my mother's side of our family. Since her mother died when she was a child and her father when she was a teen ager.

Mom's parents and my grand parents were Pinkney Perkins and Mary Jarvis Perkins. Mom had a brother Jess Perkins . A sister , Ida Perkins Pharr. She had a bunch of half brothers and sisters. Since her father had three sets of children with three different wives, having lost his first in death and then Mom's mother. The only one we were close to was Aunt Cinnie Willbanks , who Mom lived with at one time before she attended Berry School in Rome Georgia. Even though she was older than Mom , she was awful good to her and to our family.

Mom and Dad both were twenty eight years old when they were married. Mom certainly lived an exciting life. Here are some words of hers that I am coping from her own handwriting. She had such beautiful hand writing and would write long letters to friends and family. And with such details that those receiving the letters often said that it was like just sitting down with her. I received a lot of those letters before we had a phone to talk in person, and when I was in the Navy.

" This is all I know about our family in the beginning –Our Great Grand Father- Newton Judson Perkins and three brothers came to Georgia from some place in South Carolina. Grandpa (Mom's Great Grandpa) settled in Georgia and the brothers went on to Texas. Our great granddaddy settled on the left bank of the Etowah River where he raised his family.

After Pa died I went to live with Cinnie and Ezel (Willbanks, Cinnie, her half, older sister) I went to Lays school. Miss Cora Lyon helped me fill out my application to Berry(school) . I was accepted and went to Berry in September . I went the 9 months and until Xmas and stayed out and taught at Cokers Chapel that winter and summer. (In those days public schools had two sessions) I went back to Berry and was going to drop out and teach at Chapel again, but some time before the holidays, Miss Bruster called me into her office and told me she had a scholarship for me. I did some rejoicing. The DAR chapter from Mt.Sterling Ohio paid my tuition the rest of the time for me."

Here is a summary of the rest of her writing. Where she taught school, worked, until she and dad married. And taught some after they were married at Liberty school in Dawson county.

Big Springs, Cherry Grove, Payne's, Liberty across the river from Ballground, Riverdale school in Canton one 9 month term. She attended Southern Business College, but did not finish , took a job with the Veterans Administration as a file clerk and worked there 2 or 3 years. She also went to Ark and worked in a children home for four months and then came to Coggins Marble Co. She was working there when she met Dad and they married . There is more in her writings, but this will introduce you to a wonderful mother. A brilliant mother, and a dedicated Christian.

Sad Times

It is maybe odd that Mom and Uncle Jess Perkins , both lost their oldest Son in World ll. Uncle Jess's son, Quinton, died in a dive bomber crash , as he was training to be a dive bomber. Aunt Ida's and Uncle Vess Pharr's only son, Ralph Pharr, served in the army as a captain . in the war against Japan. When he was ordered to order his men under him to lead the charge with him to take a fortified Japanese strong hold. He refused to give the command. He later told us of this and said he and his squad of men would not have survived. So he could have been the third death of the Perkin's sons , Ida, Mom, and Jess.

It was on a trip when I took Mom to see Aunt Ida in Barnesville Georgia that I was introduced to golf. Ralph was playing in a golf tournament and I walked the course with him. I was nineteen at that time. I watched him, since I was a baseball player, I figured if I could hit a baseball at 90 miles per hour. I ought to be able to hit a golf ball setting on a tee not moving. So when I got back to Gainesville, where I was a barber, living with my parents, I bought be a set of used golf clubs, which I still have some of those clubs. I started playing golf, a lot at first, then very little after Eva and I married . Until I began to play with some of my preacher friends. Lots when I was in Seminary, since the Seminary owned a golf course, the Old Wake Forest course of 9 holes where Arnold Palmer played when he was a student at Wake Forest University. Before it moved to Winston-Salem, long after he became a pro golfer. We had time between classes to get in the 9 holes of golf, at least once a week, weather permitting.

Acworth High School

I spent my senior year at Acworth High School, having transferred from Dawsonville High . At first, I drove Dad's car, seems like it was a 32 model Chevrolet . But gas became rationed and tires were always going flat. I decided to start boarding with an older couple that kept boarders, about a half a dozen of us. We got breakfast and supper . I think I paid $12.00 per week. I had to buy my lunch which I did on the credit at a drug store-restaurant. Many times when I would go to pay up, since I was sorta a star athletic and had some merchant fans, some one would have already paid my bill. I worked for a five and dime store at night in their ware house filling orders for their other stores. Except during basket ball season when we had the night games.

My favorite subjects , not counting athletics, were girls.

Had a lot of pretty ones. But most of them that were pretty were already dating someone . I though that Odelle Chandler was the prettiest of all the girls, but she already had a steady . She was the best high school basket ball player I have ever seen. I saw a lot of them over the years, since I refereed high school basket ball for many years. I wound up dating a junior class mate, Pat Pope, who played on the girls basket ball team. She and I would set in the back of the bus on our way to and from out of town games. The buses in those days did not have seats like they do today facing the front of the bus, but rather benches, with bench on both sides of the bus and two benches back to back , in the middle of the bus. One of the practices was when we were returning after the games, if a car came up behind us with only one head light. If I saw it before Pat did, I could holler " Pop Eye" and I got to kiss her. Boy did I watch close. Pat liked to kiss, and I sorta like to also.

One night I had walked her home after we had gone to a movie in town and I was kissing her good night at the door.

About that time the door opened. It was her dad, he was furious .and he said," Young man I will teach you to kiss my daughter. And I said, " You don't have to teach me I have already learnt". .Just a joke. Heard about this young man who was courting his girl friend and they were sitting in the living room on the couch and he asker her if he kissed her if she would holler, " help." She said, " do you think you will need some help."

But her dad did sit us down one night and talked to us. I think he thought that we were getting to serous in our relationship. I thought a lot of her and she did of me. He was afraid that we might be thinking of marriage down the road. He had plans for Pat, she was to graduate from high school and then attend college, since he was a well to do father, as the plant manager of a textile plant. He could afford to send her. When school was out we did not date anymore. I went my way and she went her way. I replaced her with a pretty girl that had just graduated from high school in Marietta and a few others on occasions.

BASKETBALL

When the short baseball season was over, basketball season began. Our practice was the last period of school. Since almost all of our basketball team rode the bus to school. None of them owned cars, we had only a few students that had cars. We walked to school if we did not ride a bus.

Since I walked to school from the boarding house. I was allowed my Coach Cantrell to stay in the gym and practice my basketball shooting. I could dribble and guard with the best of them. But my scoring needed some fine tuning. So for hours I would practice shooting outside shots and working on a hook shot. It wasn't long till I was in the starting line up , since I could dribble, I would bring the ball up the floor , what is called a point guard today. In those days most of the teams we played, played a zone defense. We played always a man to man defense. I was always glad to see a team in a packed in close to the basket in a zone. I then had an opportunity to shoot a set shot over the zone, not a jump shot, we had the instruction from our coach to have both feet on the court when you shoot. Most of the time it was a two handed set shot. My game approved dynamically with all the time I put into practice.

My senior class mates voted me to be the best athlete in our class. All of our team were seniors but three. I remember the day when Coach Cantrell came into our dressing room and said, "your cigarettes are your uniforms, and it doesn't make any difference with me. And if I hear of or see any of you over at the canteen eating candy bars or drinking soft drinks, it will be your uniforms. Now get out there and run." He ran us around and around the court till we could run no more, in fact he did that for several days. He intended that we get in shape. What had happened. We had played the night before he came into the dressing room, Fitch Hugh Lee High and got swamped. I remember I drank a big bottle of RC Cola before the game and as I would run up and down the court I could feel it sloshing in my stomach. About a week later we had Smyrna come to our place. They were expecting to give us a good whipping since they had beaten Fitch Hugh Lee . But we had got in shape and we clobbered them with fast breaks.

I remember after that game a car full of students passed me as I was walking back to the boarding house. I had on my warm up jacket. So they recognized me as a player. And as I was walking down the side walk they passed with their windows down cussing me. I picked up a rock when they got a little distance from me and cut down at the back of their car and the rock went trough the back glass. It took them a while to get stopped before all four doors on that car opened. By that time I had made tracks, across the tennis courts and through the woods to the next street. No where to be found.

Coach Cantrell tried to get me to come back for another year . I could have since I was only sixteen when I graduated, an actually could have played a couple more years. We were at war. I had a brother fighting in that war and later died in that war. And so did James Monroe a class mate. So I went to work in a defense plant the next day after gradation. I would not have got a job, I don't think, if it had not been for Bobby Cantrell, a class mate, signing an affidavit that I was seventeen.

Bell Aircraft Basketall

I played the next season for Bell Aircraft. In fact I wound up as the coach of the team. This is how that came about. There was an announcement that the plant wanted to sponsor a basketball team and for those interested in playing to come by the recreation office. So I went to sign up and they had made the decision that the first person who showed up was to be the coach. I was the first and became the coach. Here I was coaching everyone older than me, some college graduates. But we had no problems with that. We played a lot of games that season, in some tournaments, we were a good team, and lost only a few games. Slim Doutherd , at six food eight, our center, all South West center for a college in Texas. He could hold a ball in his hand up high over his head and there was no players that could jump high enough to block it, he could shoot it, or pass it off to some one open for a shot. I was six feet one and a half inches, and wound up most of the time guarding the other teams' top scorer. Roy McClure was on our team, he had attended Acworth High School.

The Black Cat's Kitten

The black's Kitten was where some of us, boys, and grown men would hang out when I was staying with Grandma and Grandpa and attending high school , before I transferred to Acworth high for my senior year. Drinking RC Colas, playing pen ball machines, listen to the piccolo. And listen to Grady Tatum about and his yarns, about World War One. He was the owner of the Kitten.

Grady had a son, Harold. Harold was bragging how brave he was . He was about 13 years old. Someone dared him to prove it by going down to the church which was about a half a mile toward Dawsonville. And to bring a song book from the pulpit to prove he had been there. Punt Bennett who could run like a deer, and was in good shape, slipped out of the Kitten and went home and got a white sheet and ran to the church and wrapped up in it and got down between the pews.

Harold came in the side door near the front of the church and went up into the pulpit. When he did Punt started moaning and raised up between the pews. Harold bolted out the side door and Punt after him. Punt said when he passed Uncle Ed's house on his way back to the Kitten. He was hollering, " Mr. Ed, get your gun, Mr. Ed, get your gun." Punt ran him almost to the Kitten and then went to his home. Harold fell in the front door exhausted. Grady said if he found out who did that he was going to prosecute them.

I bet Harold never forget that experience to his dying day. He never bragged any more about his bravery.

Honey Bees

Dad like to keep hives of honey bees. He build his hives, which looked like a hour glass, with 12 inch boards. The bees would fill up the bottom. This would be their food for the winter. Once they had that full they then would fill up the top. We would rob the top. He would take a case knife and bend it in a 90 degree angle about two inches from the point. He could then cut through the cone and lift it out of the hive into a pan. He would make him a smoker by rolling up cotton in some cloth from some overalls that had been patched too many times. Set the blower on fire and with mouth blow the smoke into the top of the gum to drive them to the bottom half of the gum through the small crack he had left between the top and the bottom when he sawed out the gum. We never had to wear bee robbing clothing. In fact I would help dad rob hives as I got older and would not have a shirt on. If one happened to light on my back. I would tell Dad to thump it off. Best way to get stung was not be aware of one on your clothing and mash it. That fresh honey was good . Mom would make some yeast rolls, and mix some butter with the honey. That was eating high on the hog.

Bees sometime swarmed and settled in some of the fruit trees on a limb not far off the ground. Dad would get some saw horses, place an old wood door , which he had, right under them and place a new hive right under them and hit the limb with something that would jar them off of the limb just in front of the gum, which he had taken a broom and swept it with sugar water. They would go into the hive, then later in the night he would set them on the ground . If they were so high he could not jar them down, sometime he would shoot the limb off with his shot gun at let them fall. Bees swarm like that because they get to crowded, some stay others swarm and start another colony. Bees are funny creatures. The will not sting their keepers. So the keepers need to be around the hives often , and even feed them on occasions. Once in a while you could find some bees in bee trees. If you hived them you had to tame them .While I am thinking of the orchard.

I never could wait till the peaches got good ripe. I would start eating on them just after they began to turn pink. Mom discovered some peach seed where I had ate them and thrown them down under the tree. She said if she found any more she was going to take a switch to me. So I ate a few and left the seed on the tree. We had a big laugh over that.

Riding To Town In The Wagon

I can remember one once occasion ,don't remember how old I was, maybe five or six. Dad was taking a bale, maybe two, of cotton to Gainesville to sell. I was going to get to ride with him in the wagon. He was using Grandpa's mules and wagon It was cold that early morning. Since it was 12 miles to Gainesville we left early. Mom got a rock and heated it and wrapped it up and put it at my feet to keep my feet warm. I remember what the cotton market looked like. Bales of cotton all over the place. Dad approached one of the buyer and the buyer cut a big slice in the net that wrapped around the bale and pulled out almost an arm full of the cotton, then just used about a half hand full that to check the staple of the cotton. I felt like he was stealing our cotton taken so much just to check such a small amount. Of course he kept the cotton he pulled out.

I remember Dad took me to Wrights   ice cream store and bought me a big double cone of vanilla ice cream. That was some treat. After that, every time I got to go to town I had to have a cone. Back on the farm I got little of ice cream. We would make snow cream if we had good snow, and on occasions someone would come by selling ice. Mom would make Ice tea, I had no taste for it, but now love it. We also would make homemade ice cream. We did not have a ice cream freezer .What Mom would do was put the cream in a syrup bucket with it down in a bigger bucket and pack the salted ice in around it, and then put a couple of spoons inside the cream, close the lid. Then we would twist the ice cream bucket handle back and forth till the cream froze. One some occasions when we had a hail storm we would gather up the hail and use it to freeze the cream.

On the way to town, just after we crossed the Chattahoochee River . Now that road is covered with water from Lake Lanier . Named after the poet Sydney Lanier, who wrote THE SONG OF THE CHATTAHOOCHEE.

--- OUT OF THE HILLS OF HABERSHAM DOWN THROUGH THE VALLEYS OF HALL. I HURRY AMAIN TO REACH THE PLANES RUN THE RAPPIDS AND LEAP THE FALLS--

There was a step hill called Soapstone Hill. I remember one pastor we had at Liberty Church tell the story of a black farmer who would hitch his one mule to a one horse wagon with a bale of cotton in it and up the hill they would go, but he did not ride, but rather walked along beside the mule at his head and as the mule pulled the wagon up the hill, he would say to the mule " I am wiggy" He, the pastor, said. " When the load gets heavy always remember the Lord is wiggy."

Uncle Bill Cantrell

Uncle Bill Cantrell was the brother of my Grandmother Mary Cantrell Taylor. He was somewhat of a lay preacher, I remember. Don't think he ever pastored a church. As far as I can remember he lived out west most of his life. I remember once that he came to Georgia and was at Grandma and Grandpa's home. I have a picture of him and James my brother together . What I remember most about him was his skill with a 22 rifle. We would tossup walnuts in Grandpa's back yard and he would burst them in mid air. When they reached the height and started back to the ground. Also we laid a Coke Cola bottle on a post with the mouth facing him at maybe 20 feet, and he would shoot through the mouth of the bottle and burst the bottle without breaking the mouth.

I remember someone telling me this story about my Great Uncle Bill. He herded sheep at one time out West somewhere. He told of this city dude that came to visit him. There was a cub bear near by , I suppose as he and the dude were walking in the woods. He warned the dude not to bother the cub, but he did not listen. Here comes the mother bear charging toward them and he climbs a tree. Uncle Bill with one shot of a high power rifle drops the bear. And the dude said, " Can I come down now?" Uncle Bill said, "Just straighten out your legs and you will be on the ground."

I wish I knew all the things that he told us about his experiences .

I wanted to be a good shot with a rifle and became a good shot when I was just a kid. I started practicing shooting from the hip. I wasted a lot of shells doing that. But I got really good at it. I remember walking down the road with someone as we were going squirrel hunting and there was a can someone had thrown out into the middle of this dirt road. From my hip, I fired and hit the can from about 15 feet and it roiled a little ways and my second shot hit it. My hunting partner could not believe what he saw.

Bill's Brother James, and Uncle Bill Cantrell

CANTON GEORGIA

When we lived in the Bend and at the Lovingood Bridge Brick home. I always look forward to a trip to Canton Ga.

I think I probably ate my first hamburger and hotdog in Canton. Maybe I had one in Gainesville. I don't remember if I did. But I remember the Green Rail Grill. Boy those Hamburgers were out of this world. I don't know how much we had to pay for them. I would imagine maybe twenty cents each, when a coke, I guess was only ten. But like other thing became more expensive. I would also bowl at the duck pin alleys . The ball for the duck pins were a little larger than a soft ball. They had pin setters , not automatic. He would be setting up on a rail behind the pins.

We would also take in a western movie. I think it was 25 cents. Because when I was in high school and boarding in Acworth . A friend and I were planning to go to Canton and take in a movie. He and I would probably stop by the Green Rail for a hamburger. I approached Dad and ask him to loan me a dollar. I was almost broke. He said, "Billy I don't have a dollar, I have fifty cents you can have that." That was Dad, he would give you his shirt off of his back. I refused his offer. I have never forgot that offer the rest of my life. I had enough for the movie. We did not eat.

Isn't that just like our heavenly Father who offers us His only Son. And He wants everyone to accept His offer. So sad that so many people refuse His gift of eternal life?

Hawks Can't Count

A hawk can see a tinny mouse from hundreds of feet in the air. They have telescopic vision . One thing I learned about a hawk is that they can not count. Major Pirkle , and his family live about a quarter of a mile from us toward Gainesville , when we lived on the one mule farm. He and his wife, Matt, as she was called, they had three boys, Frank. Clyde, and Glynn. I think I remember that they had at least three daughters. I believe one married Utah Martin and I can't remember another one's married name. I know they lived in Atlanta. I think it was Roland , in the summer they would come back to the Liberty community. We would also come back to the community. They had a pretty girl my age. We sparked a little (bet you never heard that word describing being attractive to each other) Her name was Lorene, we corresponded occasionally for several years while she and I were teens. By- the way, Glynn and Helen were married at the same time of Uncle Henry and Aunt Lillian were.

Mrs. Pirkle had this chicken hawk that had been catching her chickens. She told dad if he would kill it she would cook him a chicken pot pie. Well Dad found the hawk's nest some distance from their home across the creek. But every time he got near the nest the hawk would see him coming and fly away before he got close enough to shoot it.

So he came up with a plan to out smart the hawk. He took me, my brother James, and a couple of others, I don't remember who they were. When the hawk saw us coming it flew away. The nest was in a huge poplar tree. I guess maybe 100 feet off the ground in a fork of the tree. I can still see it in my mind's eye. The four of us walked on by the tree and left dad behind. He hid behind the tree and as soon as we were over the hill the hawk came back to the nest and with one shot Dad shoots and kills it. In the nest were two almost grown hawks and he shot them out of the nest We came back and took the hawks and showed them to Mrs. Pirkle . That was some good chicken pie with all the rest of the trimmings with it. No, she did not cook the hawks, we got rid of them.

Santa Clause

Before I ever started to school, to the two room school house across the gravel highway. I had already in my young mind started thinking that Santa Clause was a myth. But of course I half way wanted to believe it wasn't. Dad pulled a trick on me and I guess Betty, my sister, younger than me. We had a good snow on Christmas Eve night. When we got up in the morning . I went out on the front porch and there was Santa's tracks in the snow where he had come up into our house and left our gifts and gone back to the highway. Of course it was just the opposite.

Every year at Christmas, we looked forward of receiving from Rochester New York a package from Miss Grace Fellows. She contributed to Mom's scholarship at Berry School in Rome Georgia. Mom was in the first graduation class there and received a lot of awards. It is Berry University now.

Miss Fellows kept up with Mom and our family. We loved the small gifts, but we also loved getting a lot of comic newspapers which she wrapped the gifts in and stuffed in the box that she mailed .

I remember that one year, I received a religious book from her. The title of the book is " So Great Salvation" In the front of the book she wrote a note to me in beautiful hand writing, and Rom.10:9-10.

Aunt Ida Pharr, Mom's sister, every Christmas would send us a large bag of pecans from Barnesville, Georgia, that is pecan country.

The gifts from Mom and Dad had to be limited. I guess we enjoyed the candy, fruit and the firecrackers and the sparklers . Did not need a toy. I remember I received a red handle Barlow knife which I was so proud of. I lost it
just a few days after Christmas, broke my heart.

Stealing Watermellons

As I have already written Dad never let a season go by without having a watermelon patch except when we lived in the Bend and he was sick with his foot. But we had some rich land between our house and Liberty Baptist Church on the side next to our home. I remember him telling this. I remember that watermelon patch and the size of some of those watermelons were huge. Revival was going on at the church. Someone was stealing Dad's melons. He noticed when he got up to lead the singing that some of these boys would get up and leave the church. He knew where they were going. So when they got up and left he turned the leading over to Uncle Ed and slipped out the side door and went to the patch before the boys did and hunched down in the patch. Here they came, talking to each other, " Here is a nice one" and Dad raises up and speaks, and they take off like a scared rabbit.

In that same field we had terraces that kept the land from washing. It caught the rain water and directed it to the edge of the field into a ditch. We utilized the terraces by having strawberries on the terraces.

While I am on the subject of stealing watermelons, here are a couple of funnies . A car load of my high school buddies, from Acworth High decide to play a trick on Albert " Peewee" Chance. This farmer always had a large melon patch and was known that the guarded it with a shot gun. So we got Peewee to get out of the car to steal a melon. Before he could get to the patch I ran around the edge and lay down in the patch . And when he came into the patch. I stood up and hollered at him and he took off running. I am running him some distance behind him and the fellows in the car drive off and left him as I run him down the road. He was exhausted, he wasn't in shape like I was.

I was home from the Navy and one Sunday afternoon I was dating this girl. Our family had moved back to the old home place to care for Grandma and Grandpa Taylor. Dad had this watermelon patch down below the house in the creek bottom. I drove by it and said to the girl, "There's

a watermelon patch I am going to get me one of those melons" She said, "you better not they are sitting up there on the porch and will see you stealing it." I said, " I don't care." I got the melon and we passed by our house waved at them and kept on going.

She said, " You are crazy". Then I told her that it was my Dad's patch. Then she did think I was crazy. But we enjoyed the watermelon later.

The Taylor's Country Home

BLACK BERRY TIME

Dew berries are much sweeter than black berries. They grow on vines that run along the ground are up on bushes. We had a few of these in a ditch close to our house. They got ripe before black berries. But on that one mule farm there was a black berry patch close to the fields that we owned and cultivated. On the other side of the woods that was where we raised our cotton and most of our corn. Must have been an acre in that black berry thicket. Boy!!

Did it produce some more blackberries. We would pick gallons of them, never made any black berry wine, but Mom made a lot of blackberry jelly. Black berries have a lot of seed in them but Mom would strain the berries seed out through cheese cloth.

But in those days the insect repellent OFF or nothing similar to it was available. You talk about chiggers . I got eat up, with the red bugs under my arms and other places I will not mention. Our only relief was salty butter. We would use buckets to put the berries in as we picked them then when out bucket was full we would dump them into larger buckets or a tub. It would be hard to believe how many of those berries we picked. Some were canned and pies were made from them later.

That same field must have been an Indian camp ground or something. We would find Indian relicts. Broken pieces of pottery, arrow heads, and I remember finding a flat rock about a foot in diameter with a ground out hole in the middle of it but not all the way through it. Maybe used to start a fire or to ground grain. I wish I had known how valuable those things would be now. That land in the field was rich and grew cotton real good, corn, and syrup cane, the land at our house was mostly red soil. As one joke teller told, which I have copied, " the land was so poor we had to fertilize the mail box to get a letter."

Jeff Taylor, Bills Grand Father

Picking Cotton

I remember that same field was in cotton and we were picking it. It was thick , and Mom , Dad, James, and I were picking, might been some more, probably Betty was hanging around maybe picking a little. She might have been looking after Robert in the cotton house. I guess I was about 9 or ten years old. Dad told me if I would pick 100 lbs of cotton in one day he would give me fifty cents. Boy I was picking as fast as I could. When I had my pick sack full I would run empty it on my sheet on the ground and run back. When we weighed it at the end of the day. I was short of the 100 lbs. He said you have to have 100 lbs and he would stay with me until I reached the 100 lbs. It took me until dark to get it but I did, and received the fifty cents. Now I realize that Dad was teaching me a valuable lesson.

Come to think of it, isn't that just like our heavenly Father? He promises us many things if we will do our part. He will be with us until we finish the tasks he has set before us.

Bill's Mother and children - 1935

GRANDPA TAYLOR

I was named after my grandpa. James my brother was named after Dad. Since I was the second oldest with a Taylor name, it gave me the opportunity to be named after Grandpa, William Jefferson Taylor, known as Jeff Taylor and I became Billy Jeff, I am still known by kindred by that name, later just Billy, now I am better known as Bill.

I guess I knew Grandpa as well as any of his grand children, except maybe Peggy and Jimmy, Henry and Lillian's children. Since I lived with him and grandma for my junior year in high school at Dawsoville. And when Mom and Dad moved back to the home place to look after grandpa and grandma, I was with him often.

Grandpa was quite a character. He liked to tell jokes, he had plenty. One I remember him telling about this egg sucking dog. He said this dog liked eggs so much he would catch a hen and take and put it on a nest. Speaking of eggs in a nest, Grandma had placed a white door knob in a nest as a nest egg to encourage the hens to lay their eggs in the nest. Not on the ground or some times in the barn loft, or even in the woods. A snake mistook the door knob for an egg and swallowed it and or course could not burst it . Which resulting in its death by grandma's hoe.

Speaking of snakes, Adam blamed Eve in the garden for their fall. Eve blamed the serpent. The serpent did not have a leg to stand on.

Grandpa use to tell people that when he was a little boy that the Chattahoochee river was jus a branch. When I was graduating from high school, he took me to Gainesville and bought me a real nice suit. Why not since I was named after him? Might have been the first suit that I ever owned. I think before then I only wore sport coats, and trousers. It was a beautiful royal blue one. We went to Jake Sacks' Department store. Grandpa bought all his clothes from Jake , who was Jewish . We got there when he first opened. Jake had this thing about sales. If he failed to make a sale to his first customer he would expect to have a bad day. Grandpa knew this and that is why we went so early. I picked out the suit with Grandpa's help. I remember well that he was asking $40 for the suit which was a lot in those days. Grandpa tried to jew him down and he would not budge. He told Jake he had $20 and that is all he could pay. When we started out the door, Jake stopped us and took the $20, and I got one of the nicest suits I have ever worn. Thanks to Grandpa and his dealing and wheeling.

Grandma Taylor

I am sure that grandma Taylor's children and grandchildren would agree with what I want to write about her. She was a Godly woman. She was a great cook. It was with pleasure for her to be able to cook for her family and guests. Many a preacher put his feet under her table. To eat at her table was almost like a worship service. She would expect us to use good manners and be quite as we ate. You did not talk about people. She would say, "Let's not talk about people. Maybe they can't help what they do." It did not take us long to learn to keep our mouths shut about people.

She would bake a large pan of " sweet bread" and kept it wrapped up in a cloth in the food cabinet. When I came in from high school. When I was living with them for that one school year. I would head for that cabinet.

I can remember her at church. When she would wave her handkerchief the Spirit was moving. She had such a Christian influence, if she went to a lost person in the service at the time of the invitation, and asked them to be saved. They could not resist her invitation and would make their way to the altar and kneel in prayer to be saved.

Bill's Grandmother Perkins

A Soul Winner

It is hard to close these pages as I think of the many other things that I could put in print. I do want to share with anyone who might read these lines how they can become a Christian. Or a Christian can lead a lost person to Jesus Christ.

The first thing I do, is find out if a person is a Christian by asking them if someone should ask you what a person must do to go to heaven when they die, what would you tell them?

Now their answer will tell me if they are a Christian, if not. I read to them Rom. 3:20 and 3:23 . Then I go to Rom. 5:6-7-8, and then Rom. 6:23 and then Rom. 10:9-10
Then Verse 13.

I then ask he or she, if they believe that Christ saves sinners. I ask the person if they want to be saved some day before they die. I then ask them why they have not already been saved. And I say quickly , " don't answer that question, let me tell you why. It is only because you have not ask the Lord to save you." Then I say, " Let's pray".

I lead them in a prayer of confession of their sins and asking Christ to save them. After the person has followed me in this sinner's prayer . I ask them if they meant what they prayed. Then I read verse 13 to them . Then I lead that person in thanking the Lord for their salvation.

I have seen hundreds come to Christ just using this simple witnessing tool. I call it drawing the net, in guided conversation. And have taught this witnessing tool to dozens of Christians who have used it to become great soul winners.

Bill's Grand Parents, Jeff and Mary Taylor

A Personal Word From The Author

I have only mentioned briefly my beautiful wife in the book. One reason most of the writings here have been about my early childhood and teen age life, long before I met Eva.

I was barbering in the arcade barbershop with five other barbers in the Dixie Hunt Hotel , Gainesville, Georgia. I was not busy and it was lunch time. I saw Christine Cantrell, my cousin, pass by with this pretty girl. I knew that they were going down the street to have lunch at the Collegiate Grill. I waited a few minutes and made my way down to the Grill. When I approached their booth, I said to Christine, "how about introducing me to your friend." She said, "This is Eva Satterfield and this is my cousin Billy Taylor."

Do you believe in love at first sight? Well I asked for a date soon after that. On our first date we went to the county fair. We dated often, double dated a few times. During basketball season, I was playing basket ball with Gainesville Mills Textile team. Eva would go with me and watch me play. I don't think she cared all that much for the game. But we had time together after the game.

We dated for several months before I proposed to her. We were seated in my car in front of her home in Gainesville, where she and her Mom lived. Her Dad had died on her eleventh birthday. She was born in Cleveland, Georgia and lived there at the time of his death.

I had already opened my barber and beauty shops in Cumming, Georgia before we married. So we began our married life together in Cumming. She went to work in the drug store next door to my shops. She worked there until Diane was born.

It would take too many pages to share our life together over the years. A lady with the highest morals of any one I ever dated.

The type of a lady that I wanted to be my wife and the mother of my children. One of my members told his wife, that Eva was the most beautiful woman he had ever seen. He had seen a lot of them since he was in his seventies. She was an ideal pastor's wife. Never seeking praise, singing in the choir, teaching children, winning many to Christ. A loving wife and great mother of our two daughters, Diane and Robin.

Bill's Bride , Eva Satterfield

A Sad Time In My Life

The above words had already been written when the Lord came for Eva and took her to her eternal home. Where I will join her some day. My loss is heaven's gain. But I miss her so much. She had been confined to her bed at the nursing home for almost a year. I visited her every day, except maybe two or three days when

I had a cold . Our oldest Daughter, Diane, also visited her several times each week. I had visited with her for a couple of hours in the afternoon before her death in the night. I told her I was leaving and I loved her and she whispered that she loved me. Diane then came about the time I left and was with her for a couple hours or more. She sang some songs to her. Then she sang " There is a sweet sweet spirit in this place" when Eva said " I see Jesus" . Diane said that she was looking toward the foot of the bed. Diane asked her what He looked like and she said , "White". I believe that He was assuring her that He was with her. I had quoted Psalm 23 to her a couple of times the day before , and asked if I got it right and she said yes. Then I quoted, " Yea though I walk through the valley of the shadow of death I will fear no evil for thou art with me." And I talked about those words. Life will never be the same without her, but His Grace is sufficient. I can't bring her back, but I will go to meet her. She told me once here in our home to let her go on. I asked where, she said to heaven , then she said, " I will wait for you." I shed a lot of tears.

Bill's Wife , Eva Taylor

WHAT OTHERS HAVE WRITTEN ABOUT EVA

I want to share with you what your wife meant to me personally. In 1998 Dan took a job in Monroe ,NC. I only had Ryan, he was 6 months old. I was scared to leave the security of my family and what was comfortable. I knew this was a step of faith for our family. My prayer was Lord just provide one person to encourage me. We moved into our house in Wingate,NC. We started unpacking boxes, we looked out the window and there you were mowing our lawn.

The next day you and Mrs. Taylor came and rang our door bell with a casserole welcoming us to the neighborhood. We got to talking and found what we had in common –Christianity.

I remember saying, Oh Lord thank you for providing this couple to live next door to us. Through that year and a half your wife was so incredibly kind to me. She taught me so much. She used to say Lynda , some of my friends , I feel so bad for them, their husbands do not treat them nicely. I just have the best husband in the world. Bill has always treated me so well. I am blessed. She loved you so much. She said it looks like Dan threats you the same way. I am so happy for you.

She was encouraging to me in my marriage. She was a wonderful mother. I loved hearing about Diane and Robin. She use to say to me that she enjoyed going shopping with Diane because Diane was like you who never met a stranger. She said she was more shy so she enjoyed meeting people when Diane was around. She counted the days until Robin would visit. She said Robin is such a wonderful mother and wife. Your wife, Mr. Taylor was such an example to me of what is important in life. God first, and relationships with people. She treasured her family. She was a wonderful listener and encourager.

The last memory that I have that I will never forget is the day we were moving to PA. The moving truck came. and packed up our things. Dan had left for his last day at work. We only had one car so I was sitting in an empty house with a 15 month old little boy, Ryan. Ryan has life threaten allergies to many many foods. The phone rang and it was your wife. She said Lynda what do you have for the baby for lunch? I said well, I have a few jars of baby food here for him. She said he needs something special. She drove to McDonalds and bought Ryan french fries, one of the few foods he can have. She came to my door with the bag and said here you go Ryan, you need something special to eat. I remember I had tears coming down my face. She was so kind. I knew she wasn't feeling well with her inner ear problem, but she drove and bought something special for my son. That was he kind of person she was. Very selfless and giving, and kind. She was a very good friend and mentor to me. I will always keep those memories close in my heart.

We grieve over the loss of such a wonderful lady along with you. Our great hope is in the reality that we will all be together one day in heaven. I once talked to her, after sharing about the loss of both my parents, what she though heaven looked like. She said Lynda, I don't know, but I know it will be beyond our imagination, and perfect. That brings me comfort that she is living without sickness and with our Lord.

We love you and your family so much. God Bless you

Love,
The Polto Family"

Dan, Lynda, Ryan, and Mandy
Lititz ,PA

" Bill:

Please know that our thoughts and prayers are with you and your family in the passing of Eva. My heart is sad for your loss, but my heart also has felt (from experience) the joy and peace that that comes from knowing a love one has reached their final destination –being in the glorious presence of their Saviour. I wish I had known Eva better, but the few times I was around her, I felt she was the kindest and most sincere gentle person I have ever known. Our sincerest sympathy and love to you at this time and in the future." Gayle

Gayle and Fred Birkmaier
Wingate, NC

Eva and Bill's 50th Wedding Anniversary

MEET THE AUTHOR

Some of these recommendations for me are taking from a brochure that I used to promote my evangelist ministry, several years ago.

For more than 50 years I conducted hundreds of church revivals in small and large churches, evangelistic crusades in many states and overseas. Along with my evangelistic ministry in the church and community where I was a pastor.

The others are more recent, just for this book.

" For almost all of my ministry I have known Bill Taylor as a friend, fellow pastor, and revival preacher. Without hesitation I recommend him to you. If your church loves Bible believing, Christ honoring- devil kicking , sin condemning, grace - extending, old fashioned gospel preaching. Bill Taylor will be well received as your revival evangelist."
 Rev. John Compton – First Baptist Church
 Westminster, SC

" I have known Brother Bill Taylor for many years. I have worked with him as his minister of music in two different churches. I have heard him preach multitudes of sermons, all have been well prepared and dynamically delivered."
 Gary Keener-Minister of Music- Greenville SC

" I have known and appreciated Bill Taylor since our seminary days at Southeastern during the sixties. It has been my privilege to have Bill preach four revivals in churches that I have served ."
 Rev. Vincent Wall – Wilmington NC

" Bill has been my friend in the ministry through six of my pastorates, with him preaching revivals in each of them. I have been divinely blessed with the number of decisions made."
Rev. Carl Koon- Lexington SC

More recent words from others

" Of all the pastors I have known through the years that I have been a Christian, Brother Bill Taylor is the greatest soul winning pastor I have known."
Shelby Hilton- Deacon- Kannapolis, NC

" Brother Bill lead me and my two daughters to the Lord, and baptized each of us. He was my pastor when I answered the call to the ministry. He was my mentor, preaching revivals in all the churches that I have served as pastor."
Rev. Dewitt Waters- Retired
Stanly, NC

" I have known Brother Bill Taylor for over thirty years. He has been a faithful and dynamic preacher of the Word of God for all these years. He is known for his one on one soul winning and other ministries. I have read his Christian Novel , From Riches to Rags and Rags to Riches that he has authored. What a wonderful story it is. I consider this my brother in Christ one of my dearest friends"
Roy Stallings
Minister of Music- Eastside Baptist Church
Concord, NC
Recording Artist- Soloist
704-782-9242

" I met Brother Bill Taylor many years ago. I was speaking at a prayer luncheon and he was in attendance . We became friends and have spent times together in prayer on many occasions. I have also called on him to preach for me. He is a great inspiration for our members. Even after preaching the Word of God for over fifty five years, the fire is still burning. He is a dear friend and brother in Christ."

Rev. Joe Haskett
Pastor –Grace Baptist Church
Monroe, NC
704-289-4917

Church Web Sites

Fbcw.org – Woodstock, GA- fbcjax.com -Jacksonville Fla.

Charlottefbc.org NC- Coalmountainbaptistchurch.com- Cumming Georgia.

Eastsidebaptistchurch.vpweb.com – Concord NC

Westmonroe.org   Monroe,NC

Welcometoantioch.org – Cumming GA

Mountainviewfamily.org –Highlands Ranch, CO

Shenadohahbaptist.org Roanoke ,VA

Pleasantplains.org   Indian Trail, NC

Recommending

Double "D" Auto Repair, Peachland, NC 7O4-272-8492
Highway 74 East for all your auto & truck repairs.

Marshville Propane Co, Marshville NC 704-624-4000
Quality Service on time- every time.

Marshville Auto Service –We Buy and Sell Cars
6488 W .Marshville ,Blvd. NC- 704-624-5038

Windsong Realty - Wiingate,NC -1-800-793-7380
Specializing in Growing Timber Land. NC and SC

Penegarrealty.com ,Monroe NC . 704-282-1502
Real Estate and appraisals- 1209 Skyway Drive

Grace Baptist Church- Corner of Weddington
Highway and S. Rocky River Rd, Monroe ,

Heating and A/C - Ronnie Hough 704-289-4803
Monroe, NC Sales, Services, Repairs 24/7

Bearden Funeral Home
Dawsonville Ga.706-265-3159

Dr. Joel Penegar –Optometry- 704-296-0818
1207 Sky Way Drive Monroe NC

Bonterrabuilders.com
Indian Trail, NC

Photo Pro & More- Monroe NC
1404A Sky Way Drive 704-283-5643
Expert film processing

Printed in Great Britain
by Amazon